J.M.Turner.
1980.

AD CLERUM

AD CLERUM

By

HERBERT HENSLEY HENSON

With a Preface by
the Most Reverend A. M. Ramsey, D.D.
Archbishop of York

LONDON

S·P·C·K

1958

First Published 1937
by Hodder and Stoughton
Reissued in 1958
by S·P·C·K
Holy Trinity Church
Marylebone Road
London N.W.1

Made and printed by offset in Great Britain by
William Clowes and Sons, Limited, London and Beccles

CONTENTS

PREFACE

IT IS A PRIVILEGE for one who was an unworthy successor of Bishop Henson in the See of Durham to be associated with a new edition of *Ad Clerum*, appearing as it does some ten years after the Bishop's death and twenty years after its first publication. It is indeed significant that of all the writings of his episcopate the first to be reissued is a volume of Ordination Charges. While the Church as a whole knew Herbert Hensley Henson as a controversialist and both feared and relished his pungent polemics, those who were brought nearest to him in his episcopal character cherished most of all his pastoral wisdom and sympathy. He had himself a special devotion to two pastoral classics of old time, *The Country Parson* of George Herbert and *The Reformed Pastor* of Richard Baxter; and his own two volumes of Ordination Charges, *Church and Parson in England* (1927) and *Ad Clerum* (1937), take their place in the line of great English works on the pastoral office.

In addressing on the eve of ordination those who were to be made deacon and priest in the Church of God, Bishop Henson gave of his best. It was a large store upon which he drew: his own pastoral experience reaching back to his early days as Vicar of Barking, his acute observation of the social and moral tendencies of the time, his sense of historical perspective in the understanding of things contemporary, his distrust of stunts and causes and movements alongside his belief in steady pastoral work in the parishes, and his devotion to the

3

Anglican tradition as seen in his great predecessors in the Palatine bishopric—Cosin, Butler, Lighfoot. He addressed his future clergy as one who knew the community and the climate wherein their ministry was to be spent, and he would leave them with no illusions about these. But he knew enough of the catastrophic happenings of the past to say *O passi graviora* and to draw from history "a cordial for drooping courage".

In the present volume Bishop Henson included, besides the series of Ordination Charges, the last of his Visitation Charges to the Diocese (1936). In accordance with a long tradition of the see he held quadrennial Visitations, and on each occasion he published the charge which he had delivered. In the first of the charges, *Quo tendimus?* (1924) he discussed the effects of the Enabling Act upon the life of the Church, pastoral questions such as Reservation and Evening Communion, and (especially) the tendencies in Christian social teaching represented by "C.O.P.E.C.", of which he was a severe critic. In *Disestablishment* (1928) he explained his new-found conviction that the rejection of the Revised Prayer Book by the House of Commons together with many social and religious changes in the community had made the establishment of the Church of England an anachronism. The next of the charges was *The Oxford Groups* (1932), with its trenchant analysis of a movement whose claims and extravagances filled him with horror. The last of the charges, published not separately but within *Ad Clerum*, is briefer than the others, and it contains the condensed wisdom of an analysis of the changing state of religion in the North-East of England. It is characteristic that while the series of Visitation Charges is concerned with questions whose range is as wide as the Church and the nation as a whole, each of them gives much space to reflections drawn directly from conditions in the Diocese of Durham. His views on the big questions in Church and State came not from *a priori* theories but from a realism which pastoral knowledge and pastoral duty had given him.

Controversy indeed loomed large in Hensley Henson's episcopate. In one of the addresses included in *Church and Parson in England* he takes "controversy" for his subject, assuming its inevitability in the life of a Christian minister and giving counsel as to how the man involved in it may retain fairness, self-criticism, proportion, and integrity. Henson's controversies saw him isolated from the prevailing fashions of thought. He was always a protagonist of the rights of theological liberalism within the Church: but early in his time as Bishop of Durham he drew away from the "modernist movement" through a conviction that it was ceasing to be faithful to the Apostolic estimate of the person of our Lord. He joined issue with the Anglo-Catholic movement which he viewed as a disturbance of the historic conception of Anglicanism. He offended the Evangelicals by his criticism of Patronage Trusts and by epigrams which he released in the debates on Prayer Book revision. He had no sympathy with socialism or feminism. He gave no encouragement to retreats (the aim of which he perhaps misunderstood) nor parochial missions. And there were few who followed him in his conversion to Disestablishment. Yet this isolation from contemporary fashions has not diminished his influence. Its secret lay in things far deeper than contemporary fashions: his hold upon the spirit of classical Anglican divinity, his intellectual integrity, and his belief in the power and permanence of that pastoral

duty which the Prayer Book lays upon the ministry of
the Church.

The Diocese found him always formidable, and as
time passed yet more lovable. If sometimes his tongue
was biting, his heart was warm and affectionate. To
"answer him back" was often a sure way to trust and
friendship. There was no limit to his kindness to those
who needed sympathy and help. Amongst the many
personal relations which the office of a Bishop brings,
none meant more to him than the bond with those
whom he ordained; and no days in the year were to
him more moving than the days of the Ordinations.
These were held at Trinity and Advent in the Cathedral,
and at Michaelmas (deacons alone) in S. Peter's-
Chapel-within-Auckland-Castle—that most lovely of
all episcopal chapels, which Cosin created from the
medieval banqueting hall, and where Cosin, Lightfoot,
and Westcott lie buried.

A strain of pessimism became increasingly present in
Bishop Henson's speeches and letters as his episcopate
(1920–1939) drew on. In the first years he found himself severely critical of the Labour movement in the
county, feeling that socialist policies were leading it
astray, and that the weapon of the strike was immoral.
Where Westcott had been (in a broad sense) socialist,
Henson was by temperament individualist. His courage
amid unpopularity is nowhere better seen than in his
speech to a crowd of miners at Ferryhill at the time of
the coal strike. In the latter years the tragedy of un-
employment fell upon coalfield and shipyard alike, and
the Bishop felt keenly the misery and demoralization
which befell "the finest human material in the world"
—taking his own part in the efforts to bring relief. The
frustrations within the Church, the drift towards

secularism within the population, and the darkening of the international skies coloured his pessimism the more. He was driven back upon a constant self-searching, and a faith in God. This faith is expressed in his favourite choices of a text for his sermons: "He endured, as seeing him who is invisible", "Jesus Christ, the same yesterday, to-day, and for ever", "I see that all things come to an end: but thy commandment is exceeding broad".

I end with some words of Bishop Henson which did not find their way into any of his published books.[1] The occasion was the presentation to him of his portrait at Auckland Castle. In describing some of his great predecessors in the see of Durham, he spoke of those "whose names in the record are associated with calamity and crisis":

"I will select five as illustrating my words—Tunstall, Morton, Cosin, Butler, Van Mildert. These Bishops reigned in 'evil times', and their names carry suggestions of conflict and controversy. Tunstall had to live through the critical years which witnessed the Reformation. He held the see under Henry VIII, Edward VI, Mary, and Elizabeth, and died, a very old man, as a prisoner of state. Morton had to sustain the terrific shock of the Puritan Revolution, and in his extreme old age died in poverty. Cosin, after traversing land and sea as an exile during the Great Rebellion, carried through the Restoration of the Church in Durham. Butler had another kind of conflict to wage. He upheld the standard of the faith against Deism and Erastianism. Van Mildert witnessed the passing away of the Palatine dignity, which, for so many centuries, had adorned the mitre of Durham. He lived through the first

[1] See *The Bishoprick*, Feb. 1930, pp. 61–3.

tempestuous phase of modern democracy. In future years, when I too have become a memory and a symbol, I wonder whether my name will also be associated with crisis and calamity. One thing seems to me absolutely beyond reasonable question. The time present is not less revolutionary in texture and tendency than were the times past wherein these five Bishops lived. One thing is certain, and fully illustrated by the long history which the series of the Bishops represents, that, in the great Huguenot's words, 'The Church of God is an anvil which has broken many hammers'.

"When, in November 1920, I was enthroned in Durham Cathedral and was afterwards entertained in the great Hall of Durham Castle, I remember naming Bishop Morton as the Bishop whose character and fortunes appealed to me most strongly. I read out the contemporary description of the Bishop, that he was *'small in stature, upright in person, sprightly in motion, and preserved the vigour of youth in extreme old age'*. It is related of him that, in the worst of his fortunes, when by the triumphant Puritans he had been driven from his bishoprick, and reduced to actual poverty, he fell in with a Puritan acquaintance, who, affecting not to recognize him, inquired who he was. 'I am that old man the Bishop of Durham,' was his answer, 'in spite of all your votes.' That spirit of unconquerable determination carried the Church through what seemed irretrievable disaster, and will, I am persuaded, not be found lacking in whatever adversities may be reserved for her in the future. We need not doubt it. God is with us as He was with our fathers."

Such was the man whose counsels *Ad Clerum* still demand and receive a hearing.

MICHAEL EBOR:

FOURTH
QUADRENNIAL CHARGE

December 1936

FOURTH QUADRENNIAL CHARGE
1936

THERE IS A NEW SCIENCE, or quasi-science, called Œcology, itself a branch of biology, which is being adapted to political and religious studies. Thus, to give a recent example, Professor Dodd, who has just succeeded that brilliant and erudite scholar, Burkitt, as Norris-Hulse Professor of Divinity in Cambridge, describes in his notable and suggestive inaugural lecture, how such adaptation is being effected in the study of Christian origins.

" In the closing years of the nineteenth century the development of the historical and comparative study of religions had its effect upon our studies. Attention began to be directed towards the background and environment of early Christianity. Our science moved from anatomy to œcology, the study of the organism in its habitat."[1]

In drafting the questions of my Fourth Quadrennial Visitation, I desired to provide myself with the materials for forming a true picture of pastoral work in relation to the actual setting, social and œconomical, in which it has to be carried on – in short, I desired to take an œcological view of the Christian ministry. The questions which I required you to

[1] v. *The Present Task of New Testament Studies*, p. 13.

answer, and which you have answered with care and frankness, were intended to give me a first-hand account of the environment in which you, as parish priests, are working, year in and year out, and to tell me something about the manner in which you were seeking to fulfil your ministry. How far were your parishioners taken out of your sphere of pastoral responsibility, in fact though not in legal theory, by their membership of other Christian denominations? How far did you possess, through the existence in your parish of Church schools, an effective control of the religious teaching given to the children in their regular education? How far did lack of employment affect your population, and condition its attitude towards religion? How far were the people compelled to live in pinched and insanitary dwellings; and what, so far as you could see, was their reaction to bad housing? How far did they attend the services of the parish church? How far were you able to visit them in their houses? These were questions which required answer if an intelligent and informed view of pastoral ministry, as it proceeds to-day in this diocese, could be formed. The practice of reserving the Blessed Sacrament, the adoption of the Revised Version of the Bible in the reading of the Lessons, the extent and nature of the general neglect of the rubrics in the Prayer Book, and the view taken of the parson's motor-car as an instrument of pastoral work are matters, in themselves significant and suggestive, which could not but throw light on pastoral methods and ideals, and help me to understand the point of view from which the parish clergy within my jurisdiction were regarding their duty. I have to thank you all for the trouble you have taken in answering my questions, and for the frankness with which you have answered them.

In his valuable book, *Industrial Tyneside*, published in 1928, Dr. Mess includes a chapter on "Organised Religion" which is deeply and painfully interesting. The opening paragraph must be borne in mind by every serious student of society, and is so relevant to our present discussion that I make no apology for quoting it here:

"No account of the life of a great community would be complete without some attempt to estimate the part played by organised religion. But to do so is extremely difficult. The main work of the churches is done in the sphere of ideals and of motives, and it is impossible to trace the extent to which men are what they are, and do what they do, because of the activities of church or chapel. Even if we confine ourselves to picturing and to measuring external things, church memberships, church attendances, and so on, the difficulties are very great. Each denomination has its own method of keeping records, and similar information is not always obtainable or comparable; even the two Anglican dioceses of Newcastle and Durham present their information differently in their Calendars. Nor can one be sure how carefully the records are kept; almost certainly one has to allow for a large margin of error in religious statistics."[1]

If "a large margin of error" must be allowed for in "religious statistics," how much larger must the margin be when we are concerned, not with statistics, but with personal *impressions*? The value of the first turns on the adequacy of the information which is available, and on the competence of the person who presents it in statistical shape; but the value of the last will depend on the intelligence, carefulness, and candour of the individual whose impressions are recorded. They will assuredly be coloured to some extent by his opinions, his preferences, and his prejudices. Temperament will largely determine his point of view, and disturb the balance of his judgment. I do not forget that your answers to my Visitation questions do for the most part represent personal impressions rather than detailed information, and, in considering them, I make allowance for the fact. They disclose to me how the social situation looks as you see it.

Dr. Mess's book dealt with Tyneside as a whole, including both the north bank, which is in the diocese of Newcastle, and the south bank, which is in the diocese of Durham; but the social and economic conditions on both banks are so similar that what he says of both may be regarded as

[1] v. *Industrial Tyneside*, p. 131.

broadly true of each. The population on the south bank only differs from that on the north in being poorer, more destitute of alleviating factors, more remote from public view, more monotonously helpless and hopeless. We may add that, since *Industrial Tyneside* was published in 1928, the situation has, until the last few months, continually grown worse. There is, indeed, now some recovery of trade. The Tyne and the Wear are beginning to present the almost forgotten evidences of activity in the shipbuilding industry. But the damage and dislocation of the dark years, from which we dare to hope that Tyneside is beginning to emerge, will long remain to embarrass and enfeeble the work of the Churches. Housing conditions, though still in some districts very bad, are everywhere being improved; and the time cannot be far distant when this dark feature of the social picture presented by our diocese will have disappeared. If, as cannot be doubted, bad housing has depressed the level of moral life, and formed a grave hindrance to spiritual work, we may reasonably hope that its disappearance will facilitate pastoral work. We cannot forget, however, that the process of demolishing the slums and housing their inhabitants elsewhere has created, for the incumbents of the parishes directly affected, new pastoral problems of which the solution is not easy to find. Nevertheless, we have good cause to thank God for the progress which has been made in removing a condition which degraded the people of this county, and brought heavy discredit on the nation as a whole.

The Visitation Returns of the clergy of this diocese confirm the conclusions to which Dr. Mess was led by his enquiries into the religious condition of Tyneside. We might adopt them:

"First of all it is clear that those who are professed and in any sense active adherents of organised religion are a minority, certainly less than a third of the population.

"It is clear also that the majority of those outside the churches are not opposed to religion, at least in the sense of having definite intellectual objections to it. They like to be married at church, they bring their babies to be baptised, they send their children to Sunday Schools. It is indifference, and not intellectual rejection, which keeps them away."

I am doubtful whether we can adopt Dr. Mess's statement that "there is no evidence at the present time of much further drift from the churches," for I note that many of the incumbents state that attendance at the services of the parish church is declining; but I am sure he is right when he dwells on the "lamentable waste of resources involved in the maintenance of a number of small separate causes," though, perhaps, the practical difficulty of combining the different denominational activities is even greater than he perceives. His concluding paragraph ought seriously to be pondered by all considering Christians whatever their religious description may be:

"It is common for those who care about organised religion to say that what is most needed at the present time is a great spiritual revival. Doubtless we need a spiritual revival. But to the writer of this report it seems that we need at least as much an overhauling of the machinery of the churches. We waste such spiritual power as is given to us. The churches generate more steam than they use effectively, and there is even now a sufficiency of men, of money, of enthusiasm, and of spiritual energy to accomplish a great deal if it were directed rightly and used wisely. 'We have need to cry to the Strong for strength,' said the pilgrims in Bunyan's allegory. 'Ay, and you will have need to use it when you have it too,' was the reply. The churches are not using their resources well. There are many signs of improvement in this respect, but there is still a long way to go."[1]

Without embarking on a discussion of the large and thorny question of Reunion, I must ask you to consider the bearing on pastoral ministry of what the Prayer Book significantly calls "our unhappy divisions." In three directions, perhaps, we may perceive the effect of the prevailing denominationalism apart from the obvious waste of resources, which arrested the attention of a sympathetic and keen-sighted student like Dr. Mess. First, the extent of the incumbent's pastoral responsibility is substantially

[1] v. *Industrial Tyneside*, pp. 138, 140.

diminished; next, the influence of the Church and the authority of the pastoral office are apparently reduced; and, thirdly, the character and method of the pastor's teaching are importantly affected. It is worth while to consider these effects of denominationalism with some care.

I. When once it has been frankly recognised that religious provision can be effectively made by other descriptions of Christians, then it is the obvious and primary duty of the incumbent, when he enters on his office, to ascertain what proportion of his parishioners are thus being provided for. He is required to do this both in the interest of good relations with the nonconformist clergy, as well Roman Catholic as Protestant, and, not less, in the interest of his own efficiency, for only with this knowledge in his possession, will he be able to make the most of his pastoral resources, and to perform his duty with a minimum of friction and a maximum of effect. In almost every parish a considerable proportion of the parishioners is described in the Visitation Returns as non-Anglican. Roman Catholics, mostly Irish, are very numerous on Tyneside, and Methodists are strongly represented throughout the diocese. Presbyterians, Baptists, Congregationalists, Quakers, and the Salvation Army have many representatives in the population. I think it would not be far from the truth to say that about one-sixth of the population – that is, half of those whom Dr. Mess describes as "in any sense adherents of organised religion," lies outside the direct pastoral concern of the incumbents as being definitely associated with some non-Anglican denomination. These are fellow Christians, varying in the measure of their agreement with ourselves, but at one with us on the fundamental assumptions of Christian faith and morals. With them we shall readily associate ourselves in much religious and philanthropic work, and we shall avoid as far as we can everything that suggests rivalry and mutual antagonism. All this must not be forgotten when we attempt to estimate the actual burden of pastoral obligation which the incumbents have to carry. The census tells only a part, perhaps the smallest part, of the essential facts. When I was living in East London fifty years ago, there was a parish in Whitechapel, having thousands of parishioners, in which it was generally affirmed that there were but two resident Christian householders, the incumbent and the sexton, all the rest being Jews. We must know what proportion of the people are already provided for by non-Anglican Churches before we can appraise the actual responsibilities of the incumbent. How important a bearing this consideration has on the capacity of the incumbents to carry out their duty of pastoral visitation is not sufficiently remembered.

I have already quoted Dr. Mess's belief that

"those who are professed and in any sense active members of organised religion" on Tyneside are "certainly less than a third of the population." The south bank of the Tyne has a population of nearly 400,000 – that is, rather less than two-sevenths of the total population of the diocese. I doubt if the proportion would be much larger in the rest of the diocese. If that be so, then there are roughly a million people in the diocese of Durham who lie outside organised Christianity. No doubt the proportion varies from parish to parish, but it is everywhere very large.

I would emphasise Dr. Mess's opinion that the majority of Tynesiders, amounting in his belief to not less than two-thirds of the entire population, "are not opposed to religion"; that "it is indifference and not intellectual rejection which keeps them away." We have, indeed, great cause for thankfulness that there does not exist in this country that venomous hatred of Christianity which in many continental communities forms a sinister force of incalculable strength. The crimes of bigotry, as well religious as political, have been less extreme in Britain than elsewhere, perhaps because of the longer prevalence of freedom among our people. However the fact is to be explained, I do not think that it can reasonably be disputed. Public opinion in Great Britain is not ill disposed towards the Christian Churches. The tenacity with which the

Establishment of the Church of England is maintained, in face of the paradoxes and even scandals which it now involves, is a remarkable evidence of the popular desire to avoid the open breach with the Christian tradition. But, even so, we may not forget that "indifference" is an even more formidable enemy to religion than "intellectual rejection," for while the latter can be recognised, challenged, and even overcome, the former is undefined, intangible, and unperceived. This great multitude, then, of indifferent people, often Christian in feeling, but never Christian in habit, in this diocese of Durham forms the special charge of the Anglican clergy, because they hold in the community a unique and incommunicable religious responsibility. They bring to their spiritual task the name, something of the prestige, and the property of a National or Established Church, and these cannot but carry with them a specific and considerable obligation to the community as such. It is, I think, probably true to say that the "Establishment" counts for less in the industrial north than in the rural south. The population of Northern England throughout the Middle Ages, and long after, was very small, and the parishes were very large. When the industrial movement brought multitudes to the mines, shipyards, and factories the provision for their religious needs was ridiculously inadequate. We owe it mainly to the evangelistic labours of John Wesley and his devoted followers that the people were not suffered to remain without any effective spiritual ministry. The face of the diocese attests the lateness of the Church's awakening. In many, nay most, of the Durham parishes there is no ancient church with immemorial associations to which the people look with hereditary reverence even though they rarely attend the services within its walls. The parish church is often a modern building, carrying parsimony on its very aspect, and illustrating the nadir of architectural taste, which compares ill with the older, larger, and more imposing fabrics of the non-Anglican denominations. The older inhabitants remember its building, and may have contributed to its cost. It is obvious that they will hardly be able to invest it with the mysterious dignity which certainly attaches to the ancient churches of the country. Still, even in these cases, the Establishment counts for something, and what it counts for the incumbents cannot wisely forget or ignore. Do not misunderstand me. I am not suggesting that, if the Church were disestablished and disendowed, its sphere of duty would be reduced, but only that, since responsibility must always have relation to power and opportunity, the Church of England, by possessing the advantages which attach to its present position as a national Established Church, is morally, not to say also legally, bound to acknowledge the special obligations which those advantages involve.

The parish church, as a consecrated building, has a distinctive character, not merely in the eyes of the law, but also in the belief of the people. Within its walls the majority of those who are not definitely included in the membership of the various denominations are baptised and married. The parish clergy are certainly distinguished in the general mind from other Christian ministers, and their functions are otherwise regarded. They are expected to visit the people, and in many ways to be at their service. A nakedly congregational organisation of the local Church is natural, almost inevitable, in the case of the non-established denominations, but in the case of the Church of England it is unnatural and indefensible. The fact that many of the parishioners have attached themselves to non-established Churches does not alter the character, while it limits the extent, of the incumbent's obligation. His pastoral responsibility extends far beyond the petty fraction of the people which is registered on the roll of parochial electors. He is, and must continue to be, the parson of the parish. This situation is obviously ambiguous. It is the bequest of a long history, and has survived the circumstances in which it was created and shaped. The practical paradoxes to which it may lead have been roughly forced on our notice within recent years, and have brought into question even the moral legitimacy of the Establishment itself. Disestablishment would no doubt stimulate the tendency to congregationalism within the Church of England, and would alter the legal character of the parish church, but it would not easily destroy the sentiment with which the people regard the parsons, nor withdraw from them opportunities of pastoral ministry which they will be unwise and unfaithful to neglect.

II. The diminution of the extent of the parish priest's responsibility is not the most serious consequence of denominationalism. Far more serious is the lessening of the authority of the Christian message. Religion is disastrously lowered in the public estimate by the multitude and discord of its versions. The gospel ceases to be God's "good tidings" from heaven, and becomes man's hopes and dreams on earth. Instead of confronting men with the awful dignity of Divine Truth, it tends to approach them as nothing more impressive than human opinion. Now authority is the essential mark of a Divine Revelation. What was observed in the Founder of Christianity, that "He taught as one having authority," must needs be true in measure of all who rightly claim to teach in His Name. The Christian ministry must be able to speak with authority, and only in so far as it can speak with authority will its testimony to the truth as it is in Jesus be able to win men's acceptance. But what authority attaches to a Revelation claiming to be

Divine which is delivered in many and conflicting forms, of which the number and mutual contradiction are brutally emphasised by sectarian competition and conflict? Is it not inevitable that the authority of the Christian message should, in such circumstances, be obscured, brought into question, and even wholly destroyed? No doubt it was the loss of spiritual authority caused by religious division that induced the best leaders of the Christian society to acquiesce in the essentially unchristian policy of intolerance towards all unorthodox doctrines. At all hazards, they judged, the Church must be enabled to speak with one voice, and to confound the world by the unanimity of its preachers. Toleration was the device of the enemy, for it would give free play to the divisive individualism within the Church which was the fontal spring of heresies, and thus destroy the impressive unity of Christian witness. Toleration was the weapon by which Julian the Apostate sought to discredit Christianity.

"From time to time he invited the leaders and chief laity of different Christian sects into his palace and informed them with all suavity that they were at liberty to follow any form of belief they chose – his hope being (as Ammianus tells us) that when free license was given to every shade of opinion the Christian people would be no longer dangerous in its unanimity. At such gatherings as these he was wont to cry out (in imitation of some words of his hero Marcus Aurelius), 'Listen to me to whom Franks and Alamans have listened.' "[1]

Julian the Apostate knew the Christian Church from inside; and his policy of contemptuous toleration has had many imitators since, never more than in our own time. *Divide et impera* is the formula of irreligion confronted by the truth.

The toleration which has its roots in anti-Christian policy is but a thinly disguised persecution. Only a genuine faith in the prevailing power of truth can make men tolerant in face of the inconveniences, scandals, and dangers of liberty. Because Christianity is essentially true, it is also properly tolerant. Its failure to be tolerant has ever been the consequence and certificate of its disloyalty to truth. Superstition is the parent and condition of persecution. "Ye shall know the truth, and the truth shall make you free," is an utterance of the Johannine Christ which may well give the key to the chequered and paradoxical history of the Christian Church. Liberty and truth have had a common fortune.

Liberty may never rightly be interpreted as equivalent to lawlessness. It is rather the very principle of self-respecting submission to law. "So speak ye, and so do," writes S. James, "as men that

[1] v. *Dictionary of Christian Biography*, Art., "Julianus Emperor," by John Wordsworth.

are to be judged by a law of liberty." It is lamentably true of modern Christianity that discipline has almost ceased to be regarded as implicit in membership. Denominationalism, which has reduced the Church's doctrine to a babel of conflicting opinions, has gone far to destroy the Church's godly discipline. A fretful and arrogant individualism, not content with discarding the restraints of positive regulation, now challenges the authority of the moral law itself. In this atmosphere of unchecked self-assertion, ecclesiastical order has almost disappeared. To be rebuked or expelled by one denomination is to acquire a clear title to welcome from another. I cannot find in Christian history any adequate parallel to the paralysis of discipline which now prevails in the Reformed Churches. This creates "the climate of opinion" in which you have to fulfil your pastoral ministry.

In this connection I may fitly recall to your minds the solemn words of the *Appeal to all Christian People* which was issued by the Anglican bishops in 1920. They are humble words which can only be sincerely spoken by Christian men who are penitents:

"The causes of division lie deep in the past, and are by no means simple or wholly blameworthy. Yet none can doubt that self-will, ambition, and lack of charity among Christians have been principal factors in the mingled process, and that these, together with blindness to the sin of disunion, are still mainly responsible for the breaches of Christendom. We acknowledge this condition of broken fellowship to be contrary to God's will, and we desire frankly to confess our share in the guilt of thus crippling the Body of Christ and hindering the activity of His Spirit."

Dr. Mess observes that "on Tyneside as elsewhere the Roman Catholic Church does not co-operate with other Churches in any religious activity." That Church has succeeded, though at a heavy cost, in perpetuating within its own membership the note of authority which properly belongs only to the Holy Catholic Church itself. On the morrow of the crisis of the Reformation the leaders of the Counter-Reformation adopted the policy of rigorous exclusiveness which still persists. Thoughtful students of European society like Sir Edwyn Sandys (1561–1629), whose famous treatise, *Europæ Speculum*, written in 1599, is a luminous survey of the situation, were not blind to the character and consequences of Roman policy.

"By this course," he said, "they [*sc.* the Jesuits, who were the principal directors of the Counter-Reformation] keep their lay followers in a perpetual dark ignorance of the Protestants' Faith and Religion; having made it a high degree of deadly sin, either to read their books, or to hear their sermons, or to be present at their services, or almost any way to communicate with them in religious duties whatsoever."

Here we are only concerned to note that this policy

of denominational isolation makes possible in the case of Roman Catholics a teaching with authority which is not possible in the case of other Christians. The uniquely authoritative character of the Roman version of Christianity is in England generally associated with the Irish nationality of Roman Catholics, which itself constitutes an isolating factor of great strength. Within the double fence of authoritative dogma and distinctive nationality, the Roman Catholic Church is able to resist the hostile influences of the modern world with remarkable and unequalled success. "It can scarcely be doubted," writes Dr. Mess, "that the Roman Catholics are the strongest denomination on Tyneside."

"They have increased in numbers very considerably in the past ten or fifteen years, and they are active in building churches and schools. Influxes of Irish labourers at various periods in the past have done much to build up their strength. Their birth-rate is high; it can be deduced from several sets of figures that it is nearly 40 per cent in excess of that of the rest of the population; this is explainable in part by their strength in the poorer areas, and in part also by the well-known Roman Catholic opposition to limitation of families."[1]

It lies outside my present purpose to examine the grounds of that exclusiveness of religious claim which is distinctive of the Roman Catholic Church and clothes its teaching with an authoritative

---

[1] v. *Industrial Tyneside*, p. 135.

character. Here we shall all be agreed that those grounds are altogether inadequate, and that, however formidable may be the practical disadvantages of "our unhappy divisions," they are less formidable than the mischiefs which, in the long run and on a large view, are found to grow from the enforced unanimity of Rome. Liberty, political and religious, may be easily abused, and then it becomes the occasion of immense calamities; but it is the indispensable condition of whatever social progress is healthy and permanent, and it expresses the true spirit of Christ's religion. "Where the Spirit of the Lord is, there is liberty." In humility and penitence, therefore, for much sin has gone to the fashioning of our present perplexities, but with a resolute mind, we accept the condition under which, here and now, we, the members of a Reformed branch of the Catholic Church of Christ, are called of God to fulfil our spiritual task.

III. We have to teach with the double disadvantage of enfeebled religious authority, and of a relatively small following in the population. In some sense we may be described as having in the community the position of a discredited minority. It is, perhaps, worth noting that it was precisely at the time when the Christian society was a "little flock" in the midst of a suspicious, hostile, even persecuting world, that it realised its essential beliefs, developed its moral discipline, formulated its faith in the creeds, ordered its worship in the liturgies, and, under the pressure of controversy, built up the mighty fabric of orthodox theology. The unfriendly social and political environment seemed to compel Christians to put their house in order, and thus to confront their opponents, not merely with the unregulated heroism of enthusiasts, but also with the disciplined strength of an ordered society. In reading the history of the undivided Church of antiquity, we ought never to forget that it was always the Church of a minority of the population. Long after the conversion of Constantine the majority of the people remained pagan. The Establishment of the Church was imposed on them by their rulers. It never expressed their own deliberate acceptance of the Christian religion. In spite of its State-given dominance, and in spite of its ability to stamp a Christian aspect on the imperial society, the Church was never wholly unconscious of its weakness. It did not cease to be evangelistic when it became supreme. Interpretation and government proceeded together. In many respects the position of the modern Church is coming to resemble that of the Church of the Roman Empire. In both cases Christians are but a minority of the population, and, though it is of course true that the ground assumptions of modern thinking are largely drawn from Christian sources, it is becoming daily more apparent that the ideas and ideals of secularised Christendom are not less opposed to the principles of Christianity than were those of pagan and semi-pagan Rome. The masses of the people, long dumb and unheeded, have now become vocal and dominant. If it be true that their advance to power has been facilitated by the democratic affinities of the Christian religion, it is not less true that they have never been effectively Christianised, and that their social and political ambitions have slight reference to Christian faith and morals. The direction of the secularising movement is already apparent, and its pace is visibly quickening. That direction is confessedly away from the tradition of Christendom, and its accelerating pace is quite evidently bringing the Church into view of direct conflict with the modern world. We can then no longer count upon the respect with which ecclesiastical office was once regarded, nor can we any longer take for granted that agreement in the fundamental assumptions of faith and morals which once existed. We work ever against a background of eager, resourceful, and aggressive secularism. This is a difficult situation, and cannot but affect importantly the range, type, and method of our pastoral efforts. If, then, we are, as Christian teachers, handicapped by an ill tradition, and regarded with considerable suspicion, it is a matter of prudence as well as of charity that we should exert ourselves to break with the one, and to disprove the other. We are, surely, bound in the interest of our spiritual message to bring our accustomed procedures under the criticism of our acknowledged principles, and to cleanse our pastoral methods of whatever in them is apparently inconsistent with our professed character as ministers of Christ. "Take thought for things honourable in the sight of all men," writes S. Paul, indicating clearly that in his belief the general estimate of what is "honourable" is trustworthy. He bids us, in short, to have a careful regard to the general conscience. No one would imagine that S. Paul was likely to identify the general conscience with what is called "public opinion." He was the bravest and most independent of Christians, and never hesitated to provoke against himself the full tide of popular hostility when his principles and the integrity of his spiritual message were at stake.

Read the wonderful address to the presbyters of Asia on the beach at Miletus, and note how manly and valorous a spirit it discloses: " Ye yourselves know, from the first day that I set foot in Asia, after what manner I was with you all the time, serving the Lord with all lowliness of mind, and with tears, and with trials which befell me by the plots of the Jews: how that I shrank not from declaring unto you anything that was profitable, and teaching you publicly, and from house to house, testifying both to Jews and to Greeks repentance toward God, and faith toward our Lord Jesus Christ." Public opinion

B

rises and falls with the disconcerting rapidity of a
mountain torrent which in the morning is a formidable river, and by nightfall has shrunk to a
petty stream. It is powerful to destroy, but, for all
the purposes of civilised life, it is powerless to serve.
The general conscience is a river which has its
fontal spring in the far-distant hills, and is fed by a
thousand tributary streams, moving silently forward,
marking boundaries, serving cities, carrying men
and merchandise to and from the ocean. Now it
cannot be denied, and may never be wisely forgotten, that the Christian hierarchy (which is all
that most men mean when they speak of the Church)
is ever tending to fall out of accord with the general
conscience, and not rarely has fallen so far as to
provoke against itself the most vehement antagonism.
The frightful hatreds which stain revolutions with
their worst crimes have an explanation in a long
preparatory process of alienation which has finally
deprived the clergy of all effective hold on the
general conscience. That was certainly true at the
end of the Middle Ages, and again at the French
Revolution, and yesterday in Russia, and to-day in
Spain. The fact can never justify, but it can always
explain, the crimes of crisis.

Not less serious than the suspicions and prejudices
of the non-religious majority of the population is the
ignorance of the Christian religion which prevails,
not only in that non-religious majority, but also

among those who in any serious sense "profess and call themselves Christians." Pastoral ministry cannot be unaffected by the fact that the teaching function of the pastor has now almost ceased to be effectively exercised. Historically, the two principal instruments of pastoral teaching have been the school and the sermon, and both of these are now largely withdrawn. Neither the school nor the sermon retains its former and rightful importance as an instrument by which the Christian religion can be effectively taught. It is no part of my present purpose to discuss the educational policy of the Church. That is a subject which has now acquired a character of painful urgency, but it lies outside my present argument. But an œcological view of modern pastorate cannot ignore so important a factor as the ignorance of Christian faith and morals which is now observable in all classes, and is affecting most potently and most mischievously the procedure of the clergy. If sermons are no longer to be fairly described as effective instruments of religious teaching, being too often little more than improvisations on popular themes, echoes from the secular Press, or sentimental appeals for ecclesiastical and philanthropic causes, and always so brief as to preclude the serious handling of any religious doctrine, the explanation is to be found mainly in the preferences of the congregations. They neither know enough to care for, nor care enough to listen to, sustained theological and ethical argument. Their ignorance of the Scriptures robs the preacher of his traditional method, and their obsession with secular interests leaves little attention for "the things of the spirit." In short, the secularisation of modern society has invaded the Churches, and goes far to determine the tone and temper of pastoral ministry. "Serving of tables," put aside by the Apostles as inconsistent with a full-time spiritual ministry, has in the modern Church grown to be the cardinal business of the parochial incumbents.

Viewed œcologically, therefore, the pastoral ministry of the Church of England is seen to be in many ways restricted, timid, and embarrassed. Denominationalism limits its range, lessens its authority, and confuses its procedure. It is no light evidence of its intrinsic worth and vigour that, in spite of the disadvantages which shadow its course, it yet succeeds in retaining so strong a hold on the trust and affection of the people. For I hold it to be beyond reasonable question that the hold of the parochial clergy on the trust and affection of their parishioners is remarkably strong. In spite of much belittling and unfriendly comment in the Press and in popular novels, the ordinary Englishman holds the parson in high regard, reposes trust in his integrity, takes for granted his unselfishness, and turns to him naturally in perplexity and trouble. Nor is the parson often unworthy of this unconfessed homage. There are, alas, many, too many, *idle* clergymen: there are some black sheep: there are many insufficiently educated; and a few who seem to look on their sacred duty with actual dislike. But, remembering all this with shame and sorrow, nowise desirous of concealing what is blameworthy, and desiring at all hazards to see the facts as they are, I should be false to what I have observed and known in the course of a long ministry, which now draws to its close, if I did not say openly that the parish clergy, fairly judged and their difficulties equitably weighed, do, in my deliberate judgment, deserve well of the English people, and serve them, year in and year out, with unselfish and ill-requited devotion.

SERMON

Preached in Durham Cathedral
at the Trinity Ordination
May 23rd, 1937

I am in the midst of you as he that serveth.

S. LUKE xxii. 27

ὡς ὁ διακονῶν. Our Divine Master thus describes the position which He had chosen as His own in that brief ministry which the Apostles were called to witness, and, in some measure, to share. In the Fourth Gospel we are told that the Lord illustrated His words by action which disclosed their meaning: "So when He had washed their feet, and taken His garments, and sat down again, He said unto them, Know ye what I have done to you? Ye call Me Master and Lord: and ye say well; for so I am. If I then, the Lord and the Master, have washed your feet, ye also ought to wash one another's feet. For I have given you an example; that ye also should do as I have done to you."

In the Upper Room on Easter evening, when the risen Saviour came wondrously to the disciples, He gave them the commission in words which identified their ministry with His own: "As the Father hath sent Me, even so send I you." They must so fulfil their duty as to be able honestly to adopt for themselves the words of their Lord: "I am in the midst of you as he that serveth."

S. Paul is wont to emphasise the character of
service which inheres in the ordained ministry by
employing a yet humbler word than διάκονος. He
calls himself the δοῦλος χριστοῦ: Christ's bond-
slave; and not Christ's only, but, for Christ's sake,
the bond-slave of Christ's people. "We preach not
ourselves but Christ Jesus as Lord, and ourselves as
your bond-servants (δοῦλοι) for Jesus' sake." The
original purpose of the diaconate was service in the
most literal and prosaic sense. The Seven were
chosen and ordained to take charge of "the daily
ministration," and thus to relieve the Apostles from
"forsaking the word of God and serving tables."
Bishop Lightfoot has pointed out how,

"partly from the circumstances of their position, partly
from the personal character of those first appointed, the
deacons at once assumed a prominence which is not
indicated in the original creation of the office."

The loyal fulfilment of his proper task will certainly bring to the deacon many opportunities of
spiritual service; and it is apparent that there are
individuals who may fitly, even during their diaconate, be entrusted with teaching and preaching.
Yet surely it is to be regretted that these higher tasks
should be imposed on the newly ordained deacon
almost as a matter of course. The emphasis which
the ordinal places on the bishop's licence, as the
condition under which preaching is to be included

in the deacon's duty, is hardly justified in fact, since in the modern Church the issue of the licence to preach is granted without exception, and (save for the properly sacerdotal functions) the deacon enters at once on those duties of the ministry which are most exacting, and which do certainly demand for their due exercise a measure of knowledge and experience which can hardly be looked for in men who are but just ordained. I wish it were otherwise ordered in the Church of England, so that the diaconate could be made a real apprenticeship to the priesthood. If ordination to the diaconate were conferred at a somewhat earlier age, say twenty-one, and an interval of not less than three years had to separate the diaconate from the priesthood, such a real apprenticeship might be secured. As matters stand now, it is the case that – as our Swedish critics are not slow to perceive – the diaconate in the Church of England is hardly more than nominal. It needs not, then, that I should now distinguish between the duties of deacons and priests since, in practice and in the popular view, their pastoral tasks will be almost identical.

It is of the Christian ministry itself that I desire to speak now, and to insist that, since it is properly the continuation of the ministry of Christ, it also must be, in its essence, a ministry of service. S. Paul's words which I have just quoted hold true of all genuine Christian pastors. They, like the Apostle, must acknowledge a twofold commission. On the one hand, they are charged to proclaim the Lordship of Jesus over mankind, and, on the other hand, they are themselves to illustrate that Lordship by serving others for Jesus' sake. The two elements of their sacred duty may not be severed. It is only by holding the two together that either can be rightly fulfilled. To preach and not to serve is not really to preach at all: for it is distinctive of Christ's religion that it requires a harmony of word and deed. He, and He alone of religious teachers, could offer His own conduct as the illustration of His teaching, summing up His moral demand in the summons, "Follow Me." But in our case also, if we would, in any sense, be worthy of our calling, there must be a congruity of life and doctrine. To preach a Lordship of Jesus which is not expressed in a loving service of His people is to be self-condemned to failure. It is indeed true, as the comfortable Article asserts, that "the unworthiness of the ministers hinders not the effect of the Sacrament," but it is not less true (as experience from the first has shown) that men will not long consent to receive the Sacrament from the hands of ministers whose unworthiness offends them. The fatal severance between preaching and practice was never so easy as it is to-day, when the old closeness of neighbourhood, which marked the smaller and more stable communities of the past, has mostly disappeared.

The popular preacher is replacing the pastor, and his reputation is the more quickly gained since it is free from the difficult but salutary necessity of being built on personal knowledge of the man himself. Wireless creates reputations which have no other foundation than the words which it transmits. Those who "listen in" do not, and cannot, know the preacher himself, and therefore they must needs receive his eloquent words without the running commentary of his daily habit. Yet if there be discord between the two, what for the preacher can be the real value of such ministry? "If I speak with the tongues of men and of angels, but have not love, I am become sounding brass, or a clanging cymbal."

Your case, happily, will be different. It is the case of the English clergyman that he must normally present his public ministry in the light of his private behaviour. He is required by law to reside in his parish, so that he cannot possibly avoid the scrutiny, close and even severe, of the parishioners who are also his neighbours. It is the rule of the Church of England to allow the clergy to be married: and no one who has any knowledge of human nature, or of ecclesiastical history, will doubt the wisdom of that rule. But while the parish clergyman who has wife and family widens the range of his influence, he does, at the same time, bring himself under an exacting criticism. His home is an authorised commentary on his teaching. Very reasonably does the Church include in the Ordination Vows a promise to make that commentary helpful and not confusing. An ill-ordered clergyman's home is a discredit to the ministry, and a disaster to the parish.

But it is impossible to overstate the spiritual value of a genuinely Christian family life in the vicarage. The clergyman's wife, if she accepts her duty, and seeks to fulfil it, has it in her power to wield an influence for purity, kindness, and discipline in the parish far greater than she knows – greater, I think, than any other woman in the parish can possess. Not the least part of the "service" which the minister of Christ is called on to render is that which he renders, not officially as an ordained man, but habitually as a confessed disciple of the Master, who was on earth a Servant. This service of others must always go along with a loyal performance of official duty. The claims and interests of domestic life may (and, alas, often do) become less the allies than the rivals of pastoral work. "A man's foes are they of his own household," said Christ. "Service" may degenerate into a self-dedication to what is secular and popular, and then its spiritual quality evaporates.

If the service of others be an indispensable condition of preaching the Lordship of Jesus, it is surely not less certain that service severed from such preaching cannot long retain the character of genuine ministry. To serve the people without keeping paramount in our minds the primary obligation of proclaiming the Lordship of Jesus is to enter on a descending path which must finally lead to the sterile triumph of a dishonourable popularity. In a democratic society, it is but too easy to mistake the meaning, and overestimate the value, of popularity. I often doubt whether a faithful minister of Christ can ever be rightly popular. He ought to be trusted: he ought to be respected. He may even, where he is personally known, be loved; but popularity is another matter. "Woe unto you when all men shall speak well of you," said Christ. Do not mistake me. I do not wish you to suppose that I think unpopularity is a trustworthy evidence of the Christian minister's faithfulness. We may not safely forget the warning words of Bishop Butler:

"Good men surely are not treated in this world as they deserve, yet 'tis seldom their goodness which makes them disliked, even in cases where it may seem to be so; but 'tis some behaviour or other which, however excusable, perhaps infinitely overbalanced by their virtues, yet is offensive, possibly wrong."[1]

The secularising temper of our time has not helped the clergy to be true to their primary and distinctive concern. They, too, are the children of their age, and, since that age has small regard for "the things

[1] v. *Analogy*, p. 53, *note.*

that are unseen," they easily forget that it is their appointed task to affirm the reality and everlasting character of the things unseen. Of the faithful disciple, and herein pre-eminently of the faithful minister, it must be true that he, like Moses amid the trials and distractions of Egypt, "endures as seeing Him who is invisible."

On Trinity Sunday, 1887, just fifty years ago, I was ordained in Cuddesdon Parish Church. How little I knew of myself! How little I could know of the experiences which lay before me! As I look back over that long ministry, and recall its changing fortunes, my disappointments and disillusionings, my failures and faults, and through them all the never-failing goodness and forbearance of God, I find myself repeating the psalmist's words: "I see that all things come to an end, but Thy Commandment is exceeding broad." The world has changed almost beyond recognition since I knelt before the ordaining bishop fifty years ago. This past half-century has been in every sphere – political, social, intellectual – revolutionary. But one thing remains immovable in the changes and chances of the time – a Rock in the midst of the raging billows – the Lordship of Jesus. "Jesus Christ is the same yesterday and to-day, yea and for ever." My sons, you are called and commissioned to proclaim and, in a true sense, to illustrate the power of His service, which is perfect freedom. Remember, that He who gives you your

commission can and will make you able loyally to
fulfil it, for "His strength is made perfect in
weakness."

The great historian Dr. Stubbs, Bishop of Oxford,
whom I was privileged as a student to count among
my teachers, wrote some lines in his diary which
seem to me worth quoting to you now when you
are setting out on your great adventure. They
express quite simply the spirit in which the clergyman ought to live and work:

> "O Lord, my God, I humbly pray,
> Give me Thy help throughout this day
> To speak Thy word, to know Thy will,
> Thy sovereign purpose to fulfil.
> And bless, O Lord, my work to me,
> And those through whom I work for Thee.
> Let not my fault Thy work betray,
> Uphold my goings in Thy way;
> And when I have tried to do my best
> Give me Thy light and welcome rest."[1]

[1] v. *Letters*, ed. Hutton, p. 309.

ORDINATION CHARGES

I

I am become all things to all men,
that I may by all means save some.

1 CORINTHIANS ix. 22

Woe unto you,
when all men shall speak well of you!
for in the same manner
did their fathers to the false prophets.

S. LUKE vi. 26

I WANT TO SPEAK TO YOU on a subject which is of
exceeding interest and importance, and which forces
itself on every clergyman, and never more insistently
than in the first years of his ministry; I mean, the
character and limits of the parson's complaisance.
What is meant by complaisance? We may take as
a sufficient account of it the definition given in the
Oxford Dictionary. Complaisance is "the action or
habit of making oneself agreeable, desire and care
to please, compliance with or deference to, the wishes
of others, obligingness, courtesy, politeness." Now
it is apparent at once that complaisance must be a
very important factor in social life, where its presence
will go far to determine the coherence, harmony, and
happiness of the community. The law of "give-and-
take" governs life in every association of men, large

or small. Membership in a large family, education at a good school, life in college have their value largely because they teach men, in the earlier and ductile years of life, this indispensable lesson of complaisance. In the career of every individual the mastery of that lesson is very important, for the Lord's saying never fails to find verification in experience: "With what measure we mete it is measured to us again." A man who is destitute of complaisance will be odious to his neighbours, and, since hatred is always fatal to happiness, he will be unhappy. If it be the case that a man's personal fortunes depend on the goodwill of his neighbours, then social dislike may mean economic ruin. The over-courteous, even cringing demeanour of the baser sort of shop-keepers and domestic servants, which has so often provided the theme for the satirical wit of play-writers and novelists, has its origin in this circumstance. Complaisance has been so apparently necessary to success, that it has crowded out of the mind, too eagerly set on succeeding, the higher considerations of sincerity and self-respect. Uriah Heep is the finished product of a false method, the *dénouement* of a wrongly proportioned estimate of forces. Those, again, whose influence in the community is based on the popular approval, like politicians, must needs be complaisant; and this necessary quality may but too easily come to be a habit of mere acquiescence in popular prejudices and passions, an acquiescence so facile and unconditioned that it destroys personal independence and violates personal honour. The demagogue is precisely the over-complaisant politician. Now the clergyman has affinities with both these types of necessarily complaisant citizens. He may be dependent on the goodwill of the congregation for his income, or for much of it: he certainly will be dependent thereon for the money needed for carrying on his work. So morally perilous is this dependence, that the general consent of religious men has striven, by means of endowment, to emancipate the Christian minister from mere dependence on his congregation. Voluntaryism is so plainly condemned by experience, that it no longer finds any advocates outside the illiterate sectaries, whose notions of ministry are enthusiastic, in the older sense of the word. But even if his personal income is assured, the clergyman will be dependent on the bounty of his congregation and parishioners for the money necessary for carrying on parochial work. So far, then, he is subjected to the temptation which besets the shop-keeper and the domestic servant, who sets himself to conciliate customers and employers by gaining their approbation through personal complaisance. I am surer of nothing than of this: that the financial bondage to which the Christian ministry has been brought through the extension of its social and philanthropic machinery is a fearful handicap on its spiritual witness. Perhaps not the least mischief which the economic distress caused by the Great War has brought to religion is the greatly increased importance which money raising has come to possess in the scheme of the Christian minister's life. The ardour of zeal, which promotes the organisation of new works of charity, is too little conditioned by the prudence which casts the mind forward to the time when the initial enthusiasm shall have died down, and the cost of maintaining the system which it has imposed on the Church as part of its responsibility will have to be met by the financial devices of a generation which has no zeal and little interest. I see no remedy for this grave and growing mischief, but none can doubt its gravity or its tendency to grow. The clergyman's influence will be largely determined by the personal regard in which he is held by his congregation. He has to win a hearing before his message will be heard. None will listen to a man who is uncivil, ungifted, and unpopular. Christ's minister has no other instrument at his disposal than that of persuasion whereby to induce his people to listen to his message, and to follow his counsels. So far, then, he stands with the politician seeking to persuade the citizens to accept his political opinions and to give him their votes. In some respects, indeed, the clergyman is more bound to be complaisant than any other citizen, for he has to consider the effect of his behaviour, not merely on his

own interests, but also on the interests of those whose
minister he is. He has received the "cure of souls," and
he knows that he will have to render an account of his
stewardship. That is a profoundly suggestive episode
which Bede relates in his narrative of S. Aidan's life.
It is so germane to our present discussion that I will
make no apology for reading it to you:

"Moreover, they relate that when King Oswald asked
for a prelate from the province of the Scots, to minister
to himself and his people the word of faith, there was
at first another man sent of more austere disposition,
who, when after preaching for some time to the nation
of the Angles, he made no progress, and was not listened
to willingly by the people, returned to his country, and
related in the assembly of the elders, that he had not
been able to effect anything in teaching the nation to
which he had been sent, on account of their being
intractable men, and of a harsh and barbarous disposition. Then they, as is reported, began to hold a great
debate in council as to what was to be done, being
desirous to afford to the nation those means of salvation
which they were asked to confer, but grieving because
the preacher whom they had sent had not been received.
Then said Aidan, for he also was present in the council,
to that priest concerning whom the meeting was held,
'It seems to me, brother, that you have been too hard
with your unlearned hearers, and have not afforded
them, according to the apostolic teaching, first the milk
of easier doctrine, until being nourished by degrees by
the Word of God, they should be capable of receiving
the more perfect, and of performing the sublimer pre-
cepts of God.' Which, being heard, the faces and eyes
of all that sate there were turned towards him, and they

earnestly discussed what he had said, and decreed that he himself was worthy of the episcopate, and ought to be sent to teach the unbelieving and unlearned, since above all things he was proved to be endued with the grace of discretion, which is the mother of virtues; and accordingly they ordained him, and sent him to preach."[1]

S. Aidan exhibited in his conception of ministry the grace of Christian complaisance, by which he was able to come down to the level of his barbarous hearers, to reach their consciences, and win acceptance for his message. The minister of Christ has to leave no stone unturned to win the people to the truth which he is commissioned to proclaim. He is set "to watch for their souls." If he so carry himself as to alienate them, the injury is inflicted, not only on his own credit, but also on their spiritual interest. He may become an exile in his own parish, conscious that he is disliked, and therefore irrecoverably unhappy. The people will be estranged from religion, and led to live on a lower moral plane than ever. The lack of a rightful complaisance in the Christian minister is thus always a two-edged weapon. It cuts off the power of effective ministry from the clergyman, and it cuts off the influence of his witness from the people. S. Paul is the perfect model of the rightly complaisant minister of Christ, for he could say of himself "I am become all things to all men, that I may by all means save some."

[1] v. *Ecclesiastical History*, Book iii., chap. vi.

The great Apostle's tolerance has a limit in his duty. His complaisance is not universal nor unconditioned. It is not a mere consequence of an amiable, easy-going temperament, which predisposes him in all companies to do and say what is agreeable. He has a purpose which is rooted in his spiritual allegiance. "That I may by all means save some" – there, in the governing motive, is the limit of S. Paul's complaisance. Will our complaisance tend to the salvation of those to whom it is displayed? We do not mean by "salvation" anything arbitrary, or apocalyptic, but just that raising of character and life to the true plane, which was indicated by Christ in the profound saying, "The Kingdom of God is within you." Will our complaisance have the effect of lifting men out of error and self-indulgence, towards a clearer vision of truth and a worthier habit of life? The object of Christian complaisance is not merely to please, but so to please as by pleasing to predispose towards good those whom we please, not to strengthen and confirm them in error. Will the effect be to win respect for our ministry, and audience for our message, or to make both contemptible? There is a time to be complaisant; and a time to be sternly condemnatory. "Thy money perish with thee" was the only rightful speech when money was offered for the Divine Gift. "We must obey God rather than men" was the only legitimate reply to the high priests' prohibition of preaching. You will probably all be familiar with Hogarth's pictures, which give a picture, photographic in its fidelity, of English society in the XVIIIth century. You will have noticed how frequently the painter introduces a clergyman, conspicuous in cassock and bands. He is just part of the scene, however debased, at home there, like the lay-folk with whom he is placed. He, too, is a drunkard, a gambler, a profligate, frankly conformed to the debased fashion of the time, presenting its distinctive faults grossly in himself, silent in front of its scandals, acquiescent in its reigning abuses, earning and enjoying its contemptuous patronage. It is a spectacle which merits our careful consideration. The conventional standards of conduct are higher now. Such grossness of self-indulgence as Hogarth portrayed would no longer be tolerated in laymen or in clergymen, but the temptation to be guiltily complaisant with social sin is probably not less perilous and seductive. The clergyman's duty is the more difficult since he has often to bear the discredit of opinions and disciplines which, though in themselves irrational, and rightly discarded by educated laymen, are still generally attributed to the clergy, and even regarded as properly part of their professional equipment. The world is very conservative in its religion, and holds the clergy to its conventions long after it has cast them aside as obsolete. Let me illustrate my meaning by an instance, which not only has great importance in itself, but is certain to come within your own experience.

The treatment of the Lord's day is so important a part of our general ordering of life that none of us can leave it out of reckoning. Sunday observance touches everybody, and it is probably no exaggeration to say that there is no subject which merits more obviously the careful consideration of citizens as such. The emergence of Labour as a powerful political force has brought a notable stimulus to the secularising tendency, which is rapidly stripping the Lord's day of its religious character: for Labour is everywhere using Sunday for its political meetings: and the other parties will without doubt plead the necessity of self-defence as a sufficient reason for doing the same. The passions excited by political demonstrations are particularly unfavourable to that repose of mind which a religious observance of the Lord's day requires. It needs not that I should multiply words in order to point out the serious consequences to the religion of the people, and to the work of the Christian ministry, which must inevitably follow the secularisation of the Lord's day. The clergyman is confronted by them at every turn. In society he is again and again challenged to approve recreations on Sunday, to acquiesce in the contempt of religion which absenteeism from divine service implies, to condone a manner of speaking and acting on the part of professedly religious people which is plainly irreconcilable with religious duty. He is no Sabbatarian; he is as fully aware as other citizens of all that can be urged for Sunday games on the score of health and wholesome use of leisure; he sympathises as keenly as the rest of men with the desire to make full use of the far-ranging enjoyment which the motor-cycle or the motor-car brings to its possessor. But he is Christ's servant; he is placed in society to keep the flag of religion flying in the face of the world's aggressive secularity; he is not free to let his people think that there is no duty of Sunday observance implied in their discipleship; he cannot, without treason to his spiritual allegiance and without loss of spiritual influence, allow them to suppose that, in spite of his official obligations and professional character, he approves and even envies their laxity. Nor is it only within his own parish that he should confess a duty in this matter. The behaviour of clergymen on holiday is profoundly disquieting in the matter of Sunday observance, and does certainly cause grave scandal. In too many instances they abandon religious observances altogether, and exhibit before the astonished or amused public in the holiday resorts which they frequent a spectacle of practical secularism which discredits their professed character, and contradicts their normal teaching. I cannot see how such complaisance can be defended. I am sure it is very scandalous. I hope that you will set yourselves resolutely against it; and seek to build up a worthier sense of responsibility with respect to the religious treatment of the Lord's day, a part of Christian duty which it is not wholly extravagant to trace to the Lord Himself, and which certainly comes to us with the authority of the Lord's Apostles. At least in your own persons make sure that you give no countenance to the secularisation of the day.

The best security against sinful complaisance is a religious habit, not merely – what is becoming common enough – the multiplication of formal acts of religious observance, but the steady fastening of the mind on God. To live "as ever in the great Task-master's Eye" was the principle of that older Puritanism the decline of which has greatly impoverished our English Christianity. The tendency to substitute an eager advocacy of some good cause for the self-submission to right discipline has gone far among us, and the consequences are apparent in many directions. The clergyman's life is so filled with small activities that he will be in great danger of losing his hold on the great verities of faith. I am not sure what is the best advice to give you. The difference of personal temperament is so great, the secret history of the self is so various, that it may well seem a vain thing to lay down rules of general application. Nevertheless, we cannot be mistaken in attaching great importance to the spiritual masters whose record is treasured by the Church. With one voice they warn us against the danger of a disordered life, without discipline, self-sacrifice, and self-examination. It is precisely this ordering of life which the quickened pace and multiplied interests of our time have made so difficult to maintain. May I direct your attention to one feature of clerical life which may become a hindrance to a faithful performance of duty. An increasing number of the clergy possess motor-cars of one sort or another. Let them make sure that they are not motoring when they ought to be visiting, or preparing their sermons, or engaging in some other part of their duty. In rural parishes, where the people live in farmsteads and cottages scattered over a considerable area, the motor-car may well be an auxiliary to the clergyman's work: but this can hardly be the case in the industrial districts where you will mostly labour. There the motor-car will be an easy means of getting out of the parish rather than a necessary means of getting about it. There are other considerations suggested by the possession of motor-cars by the clergy which I will not now enlarge upon, but I have said enough to direct your attention to an aspect of the matter which you ought not to ignore.

Your ordination will take place at a time which will certainly take rank in the record of the Church of England as one of the decisive points which settled the direction in which Anglican Christianity should develop. Whatever be the immediate fortunes of the

Revised Prayer Book – and I cannot bring myself to believe that they can be other than favourable – there can be no doubt that its influence on Anglicanism in general, and on the Church of England in particular, will be very great. I want to direct your thoughts to the influence it ought to have upon you who are now entering the Anglican ministry. You will have in your hands an authoritative statement on the subject which has for many years past been the occasion of confusion and controversy in the Church of England, namely, What are the limits of Anglican doctrine and practice at the present time, when the official statements have perforce to be read in the light of modern conditions of thought and life? The Revised Prayer Book gives you a fully authoritative answer to that question: I advise you to study the book carefully, and to make it the basis of your ministry. It gives you the version of the Catholic tradition of faith and worship which the Church of England understands, approves, and authorises. There is no longer any vestige of excuse for the action of any individual or group of individuals professing membership in the Church of England, and holding office therein, who shall construct for themselves another version of Catholicism, and offer it as properly to be regarded as "Catholic." There was, perhaps, a measure of excuse for such individualism when it could be truly said that the official Anglican version of Catholic

c

Christianity had been formulated so long ago that it did not take account of the new factors – intellectual, social, and political – which are distinctive of the world in which we have to live. There was even a measure of excuse for those Anglicans who argued that the Roman version of Catholicism was the only version which could be called modern – that is, which had been deliberately shaped in full view of modern conditions. The issue of the Revised Prayer Book makes an end of all such excuses: for no English Churchman can any longer pretend that he does not know the mind of his own Church, how far the demands of modernism can be conceded, what modifications of the Reformation Settlement ought to be made, and in what sense the historic protest against Roman corruptions and errors ought to be maintained. The Revised Prayer Book presents the Anglican version of the Catholic tradition brought up to date, and every man now entering the Anglican ministry cannot honestly pretend not to know what the Church of England teaches and prescribes. I charge you to give a frank adherence to the system of your own Church as it has now been authoritatively formulated, and to refuse to have anything to do with any revival of the old bad casuistry of disobedience which has brought the Church of England into such confusion and discredit in the past.

You are being ordained at no ordinary time.

Changes of momentous and far-reaching significance are visibly transforming Christendom. When I stood as you stand to-night, on the eve of ordination, the world seemed settled in its ways. Now I contemplate a world in dissolution. I ask myself what kind of a scene will you look upon when you, in your turn, have to consider, not the beginning, but the ending of your ministry. No considering observer of our time can fail to see that there is developing within civilised society a mighty movement of revolt against the whole tradition of Christian faith and morals. The abuses of Churches and the gross hardships of industrialism give a certain moral respectability to policies which are intrinsically anarchic and atheistic. In Russia the revelation of the true meaning of the revolt has come quickly. The Church of Christ is being subjected to a savage persecution, and a sustained attack is being directed against Christian morality. "The most abiding impression which the casual visitor to Leningrad will carry away with him," wrote Lord Newton, recording his impressions on visiting Leningrad in the autumn of 1925, "is the omnipresence and persistence of propaganda, 'Sois mon frère, ou je te tue!' All the energies of the Bolshevik Government seem to be concentrated upon this particular form of activity. Propaganda seems to surge round and envelop the individual like a flood." He assures us that this ceaseless propaganda against Religion is proving successful:

"Let us bear in mind that this intensive action has now been in operation for eight years. It needs little imagination to realise the effect which this tremendous pressure must exercise upon the rising generation, and perhaps it may not inaptly be compared with the effect upon the human frame of a constant tropical sun."

There is a suggestively large volume of sympathy with the Russian revolutionaries in every country of Western Europe, conspicuously in our own. What lies before us in England? That is God's secret: but "the signs of the times" are not reassuring. Nothing that is insincere, or merely conventional, will be able to stand the shock of such a time of sifting and trouble as seems to be approaching. "The loftiness of man shall be bowed down, and the haughtiness of men shall be brought low; and the Lord alone shall be exalted in that day, and the idols shall utterly pass away." We are the ordained servants of the "Truth Incarnate": our feet are set on the Rock of Ages. Just in so far as we are loyal to the great task which has been entrusted to us can we face with firmness and fortitude whatever the threatening future has in store. Be vigilant; be modest; be faithful. "Watch ye, stand fast in the faith, quit you like men, be strong." God will not fail His own; and, be the troubles of the world at their worst, you shall be sustained and carried through. Did He not tell us, "In the world ye have tribulation: but be of good cheer; I have overcome the world"?

II

The things which are seen are temporal:
but the things which are not seen are eternal.

2 CORINTHIANS iv. 18

He endured as seeing Him who is invisible.

HEBREWS xi. 27

IN THESE TWO VERSES are set out shortly the character of the Christian ministry, and the source of its power. We who bear the yoke of Christ's ministry are ordained witnesses to facts which are not seen, which lack, for that reason, the normal authentications, may easily fail to secure recognition, and may even be bluntly disallowed. We are to maintain our own hold on them, and to find power to give them authority over our own lives, because we can, by the power of a living faith, so clearly perceive them that, even in an atmosphere of triumphant scepticism, we cannot doubt their reality, facing our contemporaries, however reluctant and even scornful they may be, with the apostolic protest, "Whether it be right in the sight of God to hearken unto you rather than unto God, judge ye: for we cannot but speak the things which we saw and heard."

Now it is immediately apparent that this ministry

of witness to the unseen must be at great disadvantage
in such a world as this, must be exposed to many and
great dangers, and cannot but find itself confronted
by formidable obstacles. For evidently it is out of
accord with the normal temper of society, lacks the
normal securities of efficiency, and lies open to
plausible objections.

Look first at the disadvantages. The Christian
minister is never wholly intelligible, nor obviously useful. He appears, in the view of his secular contemporaries, an embodied paradox, and the practical worth
of his labours they find to be extraordinarily difficult
to establish. The misunderstanding, probable in any
case, is facilitated by the contradictory aspects of the
parson's life. On the one hand, he is a professional
man, earning his living by his daily work, and
therefore accepting perforce the conditions under
which daily work is measured and paid for. On the
other hand, he is the servant of no earthly master,
professes a high indifference to human estimates of
his spiritual efforts, and disdains as a blasphemy the
suggestion that "the gift of God can be purchased
with money." It is plainly very difficult for the man
of the world to fit the Christian minister into his
scheme of a working human life. How shall he
understand the utility of the Christian minister's
work? Especially at a time like the present, when on
every hand the decline of the Churches is being
proclaimed, and every gathering of Christian people

is invited to examine the problem of its own embarrassments, and to seek a remedy for a situation which
threatens to become actually unsupportable, the
man of the world finds it difficult to see any real
utility in the labours of the Christian ministry. For
naturally he applies to the Churches the tests of
success with which he is himself familiar in business
and politics, and he finds that these tests certify, not
success, but failure. On the last occasion on which
I conversed with the late Lord Oxford, he told me
that he had spent several Sundays in succession in
visiting the London churches in order to judge for
himself how far they possessed a hold on the population of London, and he had found that, with hardly
an exception, they seemed to be almost totally
neglected. What, he asked, is the natural, perhaps
the only true, inference? He left the question significantly unanswered. There can, I think, be no
doubt that there is at present a widely distributed
and probably an extending incredulity as to the
real usefulness of the Christian minister's work.
And though good nature or politeness may with-
hold, or at least mitigate, the verdict of society on the
clergy, yet that verdict has very generally been
framed, and it is not favourable.

The clergyman's work lies mostly outside the view
of his critics, who have no other knowledge of it than
such testimony as their own eyes, or the gossip of
the district, or the reports in the local newspapers

can provide, and this may be, and commonly is, neither considerable nor trustworthy. It follows that the clergyman has to do his daily work without the normal conditions of efficiency. His personal duty is largely unconditioned by routine, often lacks the oversight of superiors, or the close continuing criticism of colleagues, and can never have the sure and relentless verdict of results. In a measure which has no parallel in the case of the layman, the clergyman arranges his own work, goes his own way, and takes no account of the consequences of his efforts. In fact, the clergyman's efficiency is not assisted and measured by the factors which commonly guarantee the layman's. This difference may too easily facilitate clerical indolence, and create a shocking disregard of the general conscience. It is no uncommon experience that an assistant curate, who has worked well in that capacity, degenerates quickly when appointed to an incumbency. When the ordering and oversight of a superior have been withdrawn, he is thrown on his own resources, and these are shown to be insufficient. The deplorable revelations of pastoral inefficiency and parochial morals in a Gloucestershire village, which have been paraded recently, to our shame and sorrow, in the newspapers, point a moral which all of us ought, humbly and penitently, to take to heart. Unless there be some active counteracting force within the clergyman himself, nothing – not prudence, nor concern for his family, nor any worldly consideration – will save him from sinking under the morally debilitating conditions of his life, and to what depths he may sink are plainly disclosed in the dark and crowded records of clerical scandal. We clergy, beyond all other men, have need daily to repeat the psalmist's prayer: "Who can tell how oft he offendeth? O cleanse Thou me from my secret faults. Keep Thy servant also from presumptuous sins, lest they get the dominion over me: So shall I be undefiled, and innocent from the great offence. Let the words of my mouth, and the meditation of my heart, be alway acceptable in Thy sight, O Lord, my strength and my redeemer."

When first I came into personal contact with the English clergy as one of them, I remember saying, with the reckless decisiveness of youth, but with something of its clear vision and forth-rightness, that "the besetting sin of English clergymen was just idleness." Now, after a varied ministry of more than forty years, I still feel moved to say the same. There are, thank God! many bright exceptions, but, speaking broadly, it is the case that the besetting sin of English clergymen is just idleness.

As my own ordination recedes into the past, and I behold it through a mist of mingled memories, the saddest messages it carries are those of clerical failure, the saddest, though of course not the most numerous, yet the most persistent and prevailing:

c*

"Not hear? when noise was everywhere! it tolled
        Increasing like a bell. Names in my ears
        Of all the lost adventurers my peers –
How such a one was strong, and such was bold,
And such was fortunate, yet each of old
        Lost, lost! one moment knelled the woe of years."

It is the disregard of the quiet besetting temptations which inhere in the very conditions of clerical
life that lies at the root of most clerical failures : and
all measures of spiritual disaster are latent in the
unsuspected treasons of daily habit. If we would
continue loyal to the vows which we take at our
ordination, and still pursue the ideal with which we
began our ministry, it must be because we have
renewed those vows in daily self-oblation, and
reaffirmed our acceptance of that ideal at every
eucharist. The vulgarising influences of the world
have no power over the clergyman who thus holds
close to his Lord.

Remember, then, for your warning and also for
your comfort, that you are to be witnesses to unseen
facts, and do not wonder at, nor be excessively dis-
couraged by, the difficulties which will grow from
that character. The Cross which you must carry
owes much of its weight to the necessity of being
largely unintelligible and often misunderstood. It
has always been so. The gospel of "Jesus Christ and
Him crucified" struck on the ears of those who
heard it from apostolic lips as something crude and

cruel – "Unto Jews a stumblingblock, and unto gentiles foolishness"; and, to-day, though the use and wont of immemorial Christendom mask and mitigate the fact, that gospel, as we proclaim it still, and in proportion to our fidelity in proclaiming it, will retain its crudeness and its cruelty: for still it is as at the first, "The natural man receiveth not the things of the Spirit of God, for they are foolishness unto Him: and He cannot know them, because they are spiritually judged."

Turn now to our resources. First, we have on our side the intrinsic superiority of the Unseen over the Seen. Inasmuch as we are concerned with what is Eternal and Unchanging, we approach men and women on their greatest side, and find entrance into their deepest experiences. As we fulfil our ministry faithfully, we find ourselves receiving ever fresh confirmations of its Divineness. The pageant of moral conflict, disclosed in ever distinctive features within the sphere of every human life, comes under our view: and we ourselves become a factor in it, even a decisive factor. Some sermon we preached, some private conversation in which we took part, some chance word that we spoke, was taken up by that Holy Spirit, in whom alone we can minister at all, and made powerful for rescue, for renewal, for redemption. When once this has been realised, our ministry is interpreted and held in reverence. We find ourselves trusted and respected in a measure so far beyond our merits that we are abashed, and yet so plainly sincere that we are wonderfully strengthened. We can see that Christ has really accepted us as His ministers, and has worked through us. That vision of our acceptance kills pride, and clothes us with a more than natural courage. It is with us as with the Apostles at the first. Men "took knowledge of them that they had been with Jesus." The fishermen, as they faced their fellows in the power of the Holy Spirit, disclosed a dignity of bearing, a directness of speech, a moral insight which reminded their hearers of that Crucified Teacher, of whom men had said that "He spake with authority, and not as the scribes." The Apostles were set free from timidity, self-consciousness, and vanity by the overwhelming consciousness of their Master's Presence with them. He fulfilled His Word in their witness: "He that heareth you heareth Me." Not learning, or eloquence, or natural attractiveness, or even hard work in the parish, will bring to us this sublime and consolatory assurance, and win from the people this mysterious homage, but only that spiritual comradeship which is the proof and privilege of discipleship. They, too, must be able to "take knowledge of us that we have been with Jesus."

"He endured as seeing Him who is invisible" – the words are offered as the explanation of the career of the Lawgiver Moses. That Vision moved him to sacrifice his secular interests to his life's mission, to turn his back on the bright prospects of the Egyptian Court, and to cast in his lot with the downtrodden people of Jehovah. "By faith he forsook Egypt, not fearing the wrath of the king: for he endured as seeing Him who is invisible." This directly personal reference is the supreme distinction of spiritual religion. To the Jew it was the vision of the Holy One, near, governing, finally triumphant though at the moment rejected and sinned against, that created the prophet's vocation, and made possible the prophet's witness. The Vision came in some moment of spiritual rapture which could be fixed to time and place. That moment of ineffable experience remained in the prophet's memory as the sure pledge of his commission, and the never-failing spring of courage and zeal. "In the year that King Uzziah died," writes Isaiah, marking carefully the very time of his spiritual crisis, "I saw the Lord sitting upon a throne. . . . And I heard the voice of the Lord, saying, Whom shall I send, and who will go for us? Then I said, Here am I; send me. And He said, Go." To the Christian, the personal reference is to the Crucified Master, and for the most part the vocation comes to us in some calm moment of self-discovery, when the fruit of many prayers is disclosed, and we realise suddenly the direction of our thoughts, and learn where indeed the "treasure" of our heart has been stored. That Divine Call brings ever with it a quickened sense of personal unworthiness. At one and the same moment there flashes on our consciousness His Stainless Purity and our own unspeakable sin. Like the fisherman, when on Gennesaret he discovered the Master by the sign of the breaking nets, we are overwhelmed by a great fear: "But Simon Peter, when he saw it, fell down at Jesus' knees, saying, Depart from me for I am a sinful man, O Lord." Then to us also is audible the Word of Divine Reassurance, which absolves, and comforts, and commissions. "Jesus said unto Simon, Fear not: from henceforth thou shalt catch men." The bishop's words in ordination are the Church's authoritative echo of the Lord's words already heard in the great Silence of the Spirit. It is this secret experience on which the Church insists, and which the young man confesses openly at his ordination:

"Do you trust that you are inwardly moved by the Holy Ghost to take upon you this office and ministration, to serve God, for the promoting of His glory, and the edifying of His people?
"I trust so."

This moment of ordination, when, by the Sign of the Laying-on of Hands, the Spirit of the Unseen Master comes to commission and strengthen the men whom He has chosen to be His messengers, lives on in the memory as the unfailing spring of courage and zeal. Very movingly does Keble link

together in his intercession for the newly ordained
the fact of their ordination, and the vicissitudes of
the ministry which will flow from it. You will
know the lines, and often repeat them in coming
years:

"Spirit of Christ – Thine earnest given
      That these our prayers are heard, and they,
Who grasp, this hour, the sword of Heaven,
      Shall feel Thee on their weary way.

Oft as at morn or soothing eve
      Over the Holy Fount they lean,
Their fading garland freshly weave,
      Or fan them with thine airs serene.

Spirit of Light and Truth! to Thee
      We trust them in that musing hour,
Till they, with open heart and free,
      Teach all Thy word in all its power.

When foemen watch their tents by night,
      And mists hang wide o'er moor and fell,
Spirit of Counsel and of Might,
      Their pastoral warfare guide Thou well.

And O! when worn and tir'd they sigh
      With that more fearful war within,
When Passion's storms are loud and high,
      And brooding o'er remember'd sin

> The heart dies down – O mightiest then,
>   Come ever true, come ever near,
> And wake their slumbering love again,
>   Spirit of God's most holy Fear!"

I do not pretend to think that as ministers of
Christ you can look forward to a life which, judged
by the current standards of secular society, will be
easy or desirable. We are certainly passing through
one of those epochs of spiritual eclipse which, the
experience of the Church would seem to indicate,
lie between one phase of religious development and
another. As in ancient Israel, "the Word of the
Lord is rare in these days: there is no open vision."
What measures of unpopularity and even of hardship
may be reserved for the Church of England, in
which you will hold office, we cannot tell; but all
the omens portend that they will be greater than the
recent past has known. Certainly the coming years
will bring us all under severe testing, and make
plain what manner of men we are. In this "Day of
the Lord" there will be no use for shams. "The
idols shall utterly pass away." Only true men will
suffice for the times that are coming. There is
much, very much, in the clergyman's life which
assists hypocrisy, and makes it disastrously easy to
condone it in others and still worse in himself:

"Let the Lord's Board be railed about never so high,
never so low, never so close," writes that quaint yet

searching Puritan, Thomas Fuller, in an age which was conspicuously, even aggressively, religious, "yet Hypocrisy will either climb over it, or creep under it, or wind itself through it. The 'black devil' may, the 'white devil' never will be kept out of Christian congregations."

Perhaps the "white devil" of Hypocrisy finds easier entrance to the pulpit and the reading desk than to the pew. Assuredly we, who have the terrible privilege of standing before our fellows as the Lord's ambassadors, have very special reason to give heed to the disconcerting monition of S. Paul: "Try your own selves whether ye be in the faith: prove your own selves." But, though the worldly outlook is shadowed, and our ministry is embarrassed by many difficulties, let us not be unduly downcast. "'Tis a strange world, indeed," wrote Robert Louis Stevenson, with unusual gravity, to his father, "but there is a manifest God for those who care to look for him."[1] Yes: and those who can see this "manifest God" have gained the key to the "strange world," and the secret of its mastery. "He endured as seeing Him who is invisible" is the formula of the "faith which overcometh the world." Of this we may be confident, that "the things which are not seen are eternal," and that, if indeed we are loyal to our unseen Lord, He will not suffer us to be put to shame. The brave confession of the Apostle shall also be ours: "Wherefore we faint not: but though our

[1] v. *Life*, p. 155.

outward man is decaying, yet our inward man is renewed day by day. For our light affliction, which is for the moment, worketh for us more and more exceedingly an eternal weight of glory: while we look not at the things which are seen, but at the things which are not seen: for the things which are seen are temporal: but the things which are not seen are eternal."

III

Be not wise in your own conceits.
μὴ γίνεσθε φρόνιμοι παρ' ἑαυτοῖς

ROMANS xii. 16

BEDE TELLS US that S. Aidan was chosen by the monks of Iona to undertake the difficult and dangerous mission to the Northumbrians because, after hearing him speak, they decided that "he was proved to be endued with the grace of discretion which is the mother of virtues."[1] In his commentary on S. Luke's Gospel, Bede enlarges on this description of "discretion." He justifies it by the words of Christ to the disciples in the Upper Room: "When I sent you forth without purse, and wallet, and shoes, lacked ye anything? And they said, Nothing. And He said unto them, But now, he that hath a purse, let him take it, and likewise a wallet: and he that hath none, let him sell his cloke, and buy a sword." The Lord tells His disciples that the rule of life in time of persecution cannot be the same as in time of peace. We must distinguish between moral obligations which must always be satisfied, and

---

[1] *Ecclesiastical History*, Book iii., vi.

positive regulations which may for due cause be set aside.

"Fasting, vigils, poverty, reading, psalm-singing, prayer, labour, doctrine, silence, and such like edifying practices belong to the second category. If any one suppose that these are always binding, he will not only deprive himself of the benefits which they are designed to secure, but will stamp himself as a man of indiscreet obstinacy, and even of persistent folly."

In the hierarchy of social qualities discretion has been given a high place. It is the surest guarantee of social success. No quality is more often insisted upon in candidates for secular appointments than "tact," which implies the possession of a sound judgment and a well-controlled temper – that is, discretion. "The better part of valour is discretion," writes Shakespeare, meaning, I suppose, that the soldier's bravery counts for less in battle than the intelligent direction of it. "Discretion of speech is more than Eloquence," writes the subtle and observing Bacon, suggesting that an adroit adaptation of one's speech to the person and the occasion will be the surest way of gaining one's purpose. Discretion is the outcome of many blended qualities – patience, discrimination, a sense of proportion, versatility, self-suppression. It may degenerate into a crafty calculated complaisance, or it may rise into a noble self-sacrifice in the cause of duty. S. Paul's description of his own evangelistic method may be quoted as an example of religious discretion: "Though I was free from all men, I brought myself under bondage to all, that I might gain the more. And to the Jews I became as a Jew, that I might gain Jews; to them that are under the law, as under the law, not being myself under the law, that I might gain them that are under the law: to them that are without law, as without law, not being without law to God, but under law to Christ, that I might gain them that are without law. To the weak I became weak, that I might gain the weak: I am become all things to all men, that I may by all means save some." A many-sidedness inspired by a passionate love for souls may, as the history of the Jesuits warns us, degenerate into a politic duplicity directed to the service of mundane ambitions. A firm hold of the essentials of spiritual duty must always condition a willing and charitable surrender of religious preferences. Fuller's first maxim of "the faithful minister" unites stability and complaisance very effectively:

"He endeavours to get the love and goodwill of his parish. This he doth, not so much to make a benefit of them, as a benefit for them, that his ministry may be more effectual; otherwise he may preach his own heart out, before he preacheth any thing into theirs. The good conceit of the physician is half a cure; and his practice will scarce be happy where his person is hated. Yet he humours them not in his doctrine, to get their love: for such a spaniel is worse than a dumb dog. He shall sooner get their goodwill by walking uprightly,

than by crouching and creeping. If pious living and
painful labouring in his calling, will not win their
affections, he counts it gain to lose them. As for those
who causelessly hate him, he pities and prays for them;
and such there will be. I should suspect his preaching
had no salt in it, if no galled horse did wince."[1]

There is no collect which should more often be on
the clergyman's lips than the collect for Whitsunday,
which prays for "a right judgement in all things."
That is a prayer for discretion which Bede said was
"the mother of virtues."

If I be not mistaken the key to many clerical
failures is lack of discretion, and the common fault
of English clergymen at the present time is nothing
else. If, therefore, I devote my charge mainly to
giving you some counsels which may help you to
avoid this fault, you will understand that I have been
led to do so by a vivid consciousness of your danger
with respect to it. What I have to say may be
gathered up in five admonitions.

I. *Study your material.* The pastor is in this respect
not wholly unlike the artist, for he also is, in a very
real sense, under the control of the material with
which he has to work. He may not seek to do with
stone what he may fairly hope to do with wood,
nor attempt to make with brick what he might well
succeed in making with iron. Every material has
potencies and limitations of its own, and unless these

[1] v. *Holy and Profane State*, p. 73.

are understood, and allowed for, the ablest artist will effect nothing. The material with which the minister of Christ has to deal is far more delicate, difficult, and subtly conditioned than any with which the artist must reckon. We have to make our count with English folk, and before we can hope to influence them for good, we must understand and allow for their natural temperament, inherited prejudices, bias of place, class, employment, education, interest, inevitable points of view, probable reactions to our approaches. To ignore all these is to make misunderstanding certain, and complete failure probable. I have recently directed attention in the *Bishoprick* to the ill consequences of the prevalent clerical practice of using religious terms and phrases which cannot but puzzle, alarm, and exasperate ordinary English folk. If you provoke suspicion and resentment, be sure that you have destroyed the first condition of teaching. No teacher can afford to neglect the impression which he makes on those whom he is charged to teach. Indeed it is the secret of good teaching to be able so justly to understand the working of the pupil's mind as to be able to adopt a language which is intelligible and really informing. "Take heed that ye despise not one of these little ones" is a Word of Christ which no Christian minister can ever rightly lose from mind.

II. *Cultivate a sense of proportion.* What is it that the

Christian minister is really commissioned to do? We may answer in the words of the beautiful collect for the third Sunday in Advent:

"Grant that the ministers and stewards of Thy mysteries may likewise so prepare and make ready Thy way, by turning the hearts of the disobedient to the wisdom of the just, that at Thy second coming to judge the world we may be found an acceptable people in Thy sight."

To persuade men and women, both by our preaching and by our living, so to live here in this difficult world that, when their personal responsibility shall be brought home to all men by the righteous judgment of Christ, we and our people may be found acceptable in His sight – that is the grand object of our ministry. Everything else is subordinate to that end. The entire value of religious observances is precisely determined by their moral effect. Do they help towards the good life? If not – if, as may but too easily be the case, they become ends in themselves – they may even be mischievous, hindrances, and not helps to the good life. The prophetic protest against the multiplication of religious observances along with a low and lowering moral standard can never be superfluous in the Church. In Advent it is solemnly renewed, for then the Fact of Divine Judgment is proclaimed. How terrifying is that picture of the rejection of religious teachers which Christ draws in the Sermon on the Mount, ever to my thinking the most disconcerting passage in the Scripture, so hollow does it show all our confident judgments, and self-satisfying descriptions of our professional work to be in His sight: "Many will say to Me in that day, Lord, Lord, did we not prophesy by Thy name, and by Thy name cast out devils, and by Thy name do many mighty works? and then will I profess unto them, I never knew you: depart from Me, ye that work iniquity." A sense of proportion would make impossible most of the scandalous undiscipline which now enfeebles and discredits the Church of England. It is the lack of a just sense of proportion in the minds of religious men that explains the worst scandals of Christian history. What Christ warned His disciples would be seen in the opponents of the gospel has been seen, if possibly more conspicuously, in its advocates – "They shall put you out of the synagogue: yea, the hour cometh, that whosoever killeth you shall think that he offereth service unto God."

Recent events in Russia and Germany have brought again within Christian experience the sinister and familiar phenomenon of religious persecution. The non-Christian State is oppressing the Christian Church. The aggressively atheist State is oppressing all forms of organised religion. It is not so much the fact itself as its emergence within historic Christendom that shocks and startles us: for it implies the negation of Christendom. It is the apocalypse of national apostasy. But, as students of Christian history, we know that the worst religious persecutions have been domestic – that is, the persecution of Christians by Christians. When we ask what is the key to this truly humbling phenomenon, can we doubt that, whatever may have been the pleas, political, dogmatic, ethical, by which the oppression was justified, the main favouring condition was the failure to preserve the true perspectives of religious obligation which has lain like a blight on the Christian Church? "If the light that is in thee be darkness, how great is the darkness," runs the stern oracle of Christ. What has been thus darkly shown in the greater scandals of Christian history is apparent also in the lesser scandals of ecclesiastical life. The records of parochial controversies attest the absence of a sense of proportion. Keep steadily in view the grand object which you are ordained to pursue – the promotion of the good life – and you will be in no danger of exaggerating the importance of the ancillary and contingent factors, which alone arrest public attention, and provide material for the local newspapers. We ought to have written up in our studies, and printed on our minds the word of S. Paul – "We preach not ourselves, but Christ Jesus as Lord, and ourselves as your servants for Jesus' sake."

III. *Guard against the perils of impunity.* The English incumbent (and, in the present shortage of clergy, it is probable that you will be incumbents in a very few years) is less controlled by official authority than any other Christian clergyman has ever been in the whole course of Christian history: and the restraints of public opinion are, so far as his performance of official duty are concerned, commonly weaker in his case than in that of any other public official. The "freehold of the benefice" makes the parson independent of the people. Against his incompetence, indifference, and indolence the parishioners have practically no remedy. Only if he offend grossly against morality is there any likelihood of his being removed from his cure. The practical paralysis of the administrative system so reduces the disciplinary power of the bishop, that disobedience is easy, general, and for the most part unpunished. In the industrial districts the levels of education and religious interest are very low. Unless the clergyman acts very extravagantly there is no great probability that he will have any opposition to contend with from within his parish. This no doubt goes far to explain the fact that the "extreme" churches are commonly found in very poor parishes, where the clergyman has practically a free hand. Innovation is unchallenged and unchecked.

Impunity, and every approach to it, always affect men badly, stimulating recklessness in behaviour, breeding a contempt for discipline in the mind, and creating a dangerous self-satisfaction. That sinister quality which the Greeks called ὕβρις (insolence), and on which they held that the Gods looked with a particular disapprobation is fostered by impunity. Probably the principal cause of the abounding criminality of the United States of America is the comparative immunity from arrest, and still more from punishment, which American criminals enjoy: and I think it cannot reasonably be disputed that one potent cause of lawlessness within the Church of England is the practical impunity which ecclesiastical law-breakers can count upon. The sinfulness of disorder is not affected by the chances of its being unpunished. "Sin is lawlessness," says S. John, in his terse significant way. To a right-thinking clergyman the claim of discipline to his scrupulous regard is strengthened, not weakened, by the circumstance that, as matters now stand, discipline depends almost entirely on individual conscience and honour. Moreover, a modest clergyman, awake to the danger of his relatively unchecked liberty, will be the more careful to fulfil his pledges loyally to the Church, to his bishop, and to his parishioners.

IV. *Know your own limits.* Living, as most of the working clergy needs must, among uneducated people, who are apt to magnify absurdly whatever knowledge educated persons possess; and frequently called upon to pronounce opinions on subjects of popular interest, concerning which he really knows

extremely little, the clergyman is apt to forget the
narrow frontiers within which he is intellectually
qualified, and morally entitled, to express opinions.
The newspapers, avid for "copy," and quite indifferent to truth, will often press the clergy to pronounce on issues which, at the moment, happen to
engage the popular interest; and the clergy themselves are too often tempted, by the interest they
appear to arouse by so doing, to discuss in the pulpit
and in the parish magazine questions of great difficulty and spiritual gravity, which they really do not
understand, and are quite unfit to dogmatise upon.
The familiar proverb, "Fools rush in where angels
fear to enter," is never so obviously relevant as to
the case of such presumptuous orators. It suffices
that I should mention the many perplexing questions raised by what is commonly called Modernism,
and point to that crowded scene of clerical disaster
in which the relations of Religion and Science are
debated. The more we know – and our effort to
increase our knowledge ought to grow more earnest
and arduous as experience discloses our ignorance
– the less we shall be disposed to handle questions
which we do not understand: and, I will add, the
more our people come to understand that our
abstinence from topical preaching is dictated by our
respect for the truth, and our keen consciousness of
responsibility, the more will they value such opinions
as we can honestly offer, and the less impressed will

they be by the facile affirmations of popular scepticism.

V. *Hold yourself sternly to your own standards*. It is surely not the least of the clergyman's distinctive trials that he must ever be upholding before the people the standards of Christian thought and practice, which genuine discipleship requires us to accept. He dare not lower those standards to make them congruous with his own behaviour: but the inevitable contrast between the two will always be painful and humiliating. The touching confidence in us, which our people, often far better Christians than ourselves, exhibit, cannot but afflict us with a kind of shame:

> "Best friends would loathe us if what things perverse
> We know of our own selves they also knew.
> Lord! Holy One, if Thou Who knowest worse,
>   Should'st loathe us too.

Yet we must never acquiesce in a discord between our public teaching and our private behaviour. To do that would be to infuse into our lives a corrupting principle, and disintegrate our character. Sincerity is the salt of spiritual service. At all hazards we must strive to reach the ideals we proclaim. I think that the heaviest trial of clerical life is the consciousness that we ourselves are making it difficult for the people to accept our message. Let us not be too depressed by it: and let us never take refuge in a mechanical professionalism which obscures it, and thus mitigates its weight. If, humbly and honestly, we try to fulfil the ministry to which we have been ordained, we also may dare to say with S. Paul: "Such confidence have we through Christ to God-ward: not that we are sufficient of ourselves, to account anything as from ourselves: but our sufficiency is from God: who also made us sufficient as ministers of a new covenant: not of the letter, but of the Spirit: for the letter killeth, but the Spirit giveth life."

IV

I heard the voice of the Lord, saying, Whom shall I send? And who will go for us? Then I said, Here am I: send me. And He said, Go.

ISAIAH vi. 8, 9

YOU HAVE COME to the threshold of a great crisis in your life, the greatest surely of all the crises which you have yet had to encounter, or will have to encounter. For many months, probably for some years, this crisis has been kept before your minds as an event in the future, which you must face some day, and now you are actually required to face it. Your studies have been increasingly dominated by it; your plans and hopes have presupposed it; your behaviour can hardly have been altogether unaffected by it. Now, in a few hours, you will have crossed the Rubicon of an irreversible decision, and stamped on your lives a distinctive character. No man can give himself to the work of the Christian ministry "in the days of his youth" and be afterwards as if he had not made that choice, and put his hand to that plough.

There is not much that can be usefully said now. Nevertheless, it is fitting that I, the bishop who must accept the solemn responsibility of ordaining you, should say a few final words before the great occasion of your ordination.

The circumstance that you will be ordained at a time when the world is filled with fear and confusion will remind you that your ministry will have to be fulfilled in a society which is absorbed by other concerns than those which you represent and hold to be of primary importance. Indeed, you are entering on your sacred task in no ordinary time. A reflective observer of the civilised world might well be moved to adopt the sombre language of the Hebrew prophet as no unfitting description of the scene he contemplates: "The whole head is sick, and the whole heart faint. From the sole of the foot even unto the head, there is no soundness in it." If, to the ordinary citizen, the outlook is dark and threatening, what is it to the Christian minister? In his case all the factors of gloom and menace are reinforced by special circumstances of danger and perplexity. It is literally true that you are being ordained in an epoch of persecution. A large part of the Christian Church is passing through "a great tribulation," and "the noble army of martyrs" is receiving many recruits. In Russia pre-eminently, in some measure also in Germany and Spain, this affliction is marked by a sinister characteristic which quickens our interest with a great fear. It is the symptom of a deep-seated and general revolt against the traditional system — economic, social, and above all ecclesiastical – of

D

historic Christendom. How feeble is the hold of the
Church on the people of England may be seen by
the fact, to which much attention has been recently
directed, that, while there are more than 24,000,000
persons in England alone who, being above the age
of twenty-one years, are qualified to vote for members
of the national Parliament, there are little more than
$2\frac{1}{2}$ million persons above the age of twelve or thirteen
who are communicants in the national Church.

The position of apparent security and even dignity
which the English clergy still hold in the community
is clearly delusive. You would be blind to the
plainest "signs of the times" if you indulged any
dreams of selfish advancement and worldly ambition. The appeal of S. Paul to his spiritual son may
well be addressed by an English bishop to-day to the
young men whom he ordains: "Suffer hardship with
me as a good soldier of Jesus Christ." Harder than
the prospect of comparative poverty is the discovery
that we seem inevitably destined, as clergymen, to
be thrust outside the main stream of modern life.
It is increasingly difficult to vindicate a place for
the Church in the scheme of democracy. "The
whole system is becoming an anachronism," said the
Dean of S. Paul's (Dr. Inge), recently in his luminous,
disconcerting way; and that sense of exile is bitter
indeed – most bitter in the case of those whose gifts
and habitudes seem to disclose no common fitness
for secular success. It is no marvel that many, very

many, turn away from the Christian ministry, which
has so poor a prospect and such a straitened sphere
to offer. But you have not done this; rather you
would say with S. Peter, when the Lord, at a moment
of general desertion, made appeal to the Twelve
with the sad enquiry, "Would ye also go away?"
"Lord, to whom shall we go? Thou hast the words
of eternal life: and we have believed, and know that
Thou art the Holy One of God."

This firm conviction of the Divine Lordship of
Jesus is not to be shaken by the varying fortunes
which the world brings. It is the Rock on which
the Church is builded: it is the Rock on which alone
a personal discipleship can rest securely. "On this
Rock I will build My Church; and the gates of
Hades shall not prevail against it." Once possessed,
it brings into life an element of stability, and
strengthens character with a high and stedfast
loyalty. To have the interior persuasion that Jesus,
surely none other than He, has called us to take part
with Him in His great Crusade of Redemption, is
to be proof against the cold reasonings of mundane
prudence, and the more seductive appeals of personal ambition. "Lord, Thou knowest all things;
Thou knowest that I love thee" – that is the root of
the matter. The man who can say that, who cannot
but say that, must go forward to his ordination,
though the world were never so hostile. And this
twofold conviction that "Jesus is Lord," and that

He calls us, is the essence of our ordination vows. Without it, none of us should dare to be ordained: with it, none of us should dare to keep back from ordination. Here is the spring of our courage, and here is the source of our hope: "I am not ashamed: for I know Him whom I have believed? And I am persuaded that He is able to guard that which I have committed unto Him against that day."

Assuming, as I am bound to assume, that you will make your vows to-morrow on the ground, and in the strength, of that twofold conviction, I desire to speak to you shortly of the vows themselves. In doing so, I must needs remember that the same vows bind the bishop, though, of course, in his case with the added responsibilities of governing office. I desire to associate myself with you in some reflections on the pledges under which we, the clergy of the Church of England, receive the commission of our ministry. There ought surely to be entire agreement here between the bishop and those whom he ordains. Both priest and bishop receive a copy of the Holy Bible as the symbol of their ministry, and both are solemnly pledged to make the Bible, not only the subject of their teaching, but also the final standard of saving truth. I need not remind you of the far-reaching significance of this symbol and pledge. They indicate the historic fact that our Church is a Reformed Church, and that it accepts the governing principle of the Reformation. The paramount character of our ministry, as it is disclosed at our ordination, is that of teaching and pastorate.

You know how solemnly I, as the Church's mouth-piece, shall press on you in the course of the service the duty of Bible study – habitual, prayerful, intelligent. Moreover, we are not free to make the Bible the servant of any doctrines and practices which we may like. We pledge ourselves "to give our faithful diligence always so to minister the Doctrine and Sacraments, and the Discipline of Christ, as the Lord hath commanded, and as this Church and Realm hath received the same, according to the Commandments of God." The reference is, beyond all dispute, to the national settlement of religion carried out in the XVIth century, and expressed legally in the Established System. We must carry on our ministry as loyal sons of the Church of England. That there may be no mistaking the fact or the nature of our obligation in this respect, it is ordered that every clergyman, on entering a parish as its incumbent, must read publicly the Thirty-nine Articles to the people, and declare his assent to them. The Thirty-nine Articles are not properly articles of belief in the sense of creeds, nor are they to be reasonably applied to settle questions raised long after they were composed: but they certainly are an authoritative statement of the position of the Church of England with respect to the matter in debate at the time of the Reformation. They set forth our "platform" as a Reformed Church, and, so far at least, we are bound honestly to adhere to them.

The ordinal assumes that the priest will normally be engaged in parish work. Three of the vows are directly concerned with the performance of parochial duty, and the behaviour of the parish clergyman. His ministry is private as well as public: he must deal with individuals as well as with the congregation, with the sick as well as with the whole. Now this will ordinarily involve a regular system of visitation from house to house, conceived and carried out in the spirit of pastoral responsibility. The parish clergyman is to set a worthy example of Christian living in his own person, and in his own house. I need not say how gravely important this is, and how directly it bears on the question of clerical marriage. It is not unusual to hear clergymen complain bitterly that, in appointments, the bishops take into account the qualifications of the wife as well as of the clergyman. The truth is that the competence of a married clergyman cannot be separated from the suitability, in mind and habit, of his wife. I need not say more on this point than to emphasise the solemn responsibility with which a clergyman should marry. He is not free to ignore, in his choice of a wife, the evident requirements of his sacred duty. The last of his ordination vows pledges the clergyman to be obedient to authority. The notorious confusion in which the Church of England has been brought by the partial paralysis of its legal system, and the spread of an insubordinate habit among many of the clergy, renders this vow of cardinal importance. Let me read it to you:

"Will you reverently obey your Ordinary, and other Chief Ministers, unto whom is committed the charge and government over you; following with a glad mind and will their godly admonitions, and submitting yourselves to their godly admonitions?

"I will so do, the Lord being my helper."

That vow, sincerely made and honestly interpreted, ought to save the Church of England from the scandal and weakness of our present disorders. The difficult situation which has been created by the action of the House of Commons in rejecting the Revised Prayer Book has added greatly to the importance of that "canonical obedience" which the clergy so solemnly profess, and alas! in too many cases so lightly disregard. I am sure that you will consider this matter very solemnly, and recognise the obligation which is imposed on you.

I cannot think it superfluous to remind you, that you will move about in society as men who are in special measure publicly bound to be loyal to His Majesty. To a considering Christian man the oath of allegiance can never be a mere form. I do not wish to read into it more than, rightly and reasonably, it must imply, but at least it must be understood to mean that the English clergyman is a loyal supporter of the Throne, and that he honestly owns the Divine right of the State within its proper sphere to the obedience of Christian men. He cannot associate himself, directly or indirectly, with any movements of disaffection in society. The XXXVIIIth Article condemns the doctrine of the Communists, and every English clergyman publicly subscribes that condemnation. I think it important to say this because you are being ordained in a time of grave social unrest, when loyalty may again, as in former times, become an unpopular and even a dangerous creed to profess. It is certainly no longer necessary to warn you against irrational and fantastic versions of loyalty such as distracted clerical minds at the Revolution of 1688, but it is not wholly superfluous to remind you that our religion binds us to a noble doctrine of civic duty, and to a sincere deference to the King as the head of the State. Nor is it unreal or irrelevant to observe that His Majesty has added to the official title to our loyalty which he possesses the personal claim of a just and God-fearing man devoted to his solemn and difficult duty.

"Take heed to thyself" is S. Paul's counsel to Timothy: let me take it from the Apostle, and give it at this solemn hour to you. Your ministry will surely bring you into many temptations, which, apart from it, you would not have been required to sustain. "A man's foes are they of his own household," said the Master very disconcertingly. How searchingly true to experience those words are! From the secret places of temperament and tendency, from the subtle abiding impressions of education, from the lingering effects of personal fault, there spring the temptations which threaten us most, and which we least perceive. Probably you will be brought much into contact with boys, especially choir-boys. Avoid affectionate intimacies which are very easy to form, and which sometimes develop in ways which were far from what was intended, or imagined to be possible. I just lift the veil from an immense tragedy, which is nearer the clergyman's life than it is pleasant to remember, or prudent to forget. Avoid favouritism in work. Remember, you are entering on your ministry in the mid-course of a revolution in the opinions and habits of women. Beyond all question, there is a licentious temper now general in social intercourse which finds perilous expression in the behaviour of both sexes, but most perilously in that of the sex which is least habituated to the free movement of life in society. Your best, indeed your only sufficient, protection is the Grace of God, sought and gained in a disciplined life of personal religion. It is the sleeping soldier who is surprised by the enemy, not the soldier armed and vigilant at his post of duty.

"Set not your mind on high things, but condescend to things that are lowly," says S. Paul, with profound

D*

wisdom born of intuitive sympathy and many-sided experience. The "high things" of speculative theology, the questions about which the most obstinate controversies have raged, have little connection with religion, and none at all with morality. The "lowly things" of daily duty are those which should most concern us. ᾽αλλὰ τοῖς ταπεινοῖς συναπαγόμενοι. We are to be "carried away with" them – that is, passionately interested in them. Here, again, the little things of daily duty are to be transfigured into greatness by being seen in the context of Christ's service. It is not merely old-fashioned prejudice which makes us older men look with some alarm at the free carriage of many young clergymen in public. To smoke in the streets, to make use of slang expressions, even in the pulpit, to dress as a layman – these are difficult to harmonise with a genuine reverence, and do make it difficult for a young clergyman to win for his sacred office that respect which is due to it. I am sure they earn for him personally anything rather than the kind of deference which the Lord's servant ought to command among Christian people. There is a place for good taste in religion; and a very important place for good feeling.

Be very careful about paying your debts. Young men are often careless in these matters. To the poor especially, and to the best kind of tradesmen, punctuality in payment is a proof of character, and they suspect irregularity. You may have a comparatively small income: but you must live within it. This is, of course, the tritest of counsels. Nevertheless it is too often neglected; and the number of clergymen who come into grave discredit by getting into debt is far larger than you would suppose. "*Obsta principiis*" is a sound maxim with respect to all forms of evil habit, but never so true as in respect to getting into debt. I will allow myself to sum up these practical counsels in the familiar lines of Shakespeare:

> "This above all: to thine own self be true,
> And it must follow as the night the day,
> Thou canst not then be false to any man."

Self-respect, based on self-knowledge, and chastened by self-criticism is the key to right behaviour in the thousand situations of social intercourse. It is the very principle of "the royal law according to the Scriptures" – that law which sums up one side of human duty: "Thou shalt love thy neighbour as thyself."

You are going to be ordained, to receive a formal commission as ministers of Christ, to be consecrated by the Holy Spirit for a life of spiritual witness. If there be anything certain in the tradition of the Catholic Church, it is the origin of the Christian ministry in the appointment of the Lord Himself. However much the students of Christian origins may differ as to the form and range of the earliest ministry, all agree that it existed in the persons of the Apostles, and that the Apostles were called and commissioned by Christ. It is our happiness to be members of a Church which has maintained the ancient ministry of the bishops, and we receive our orders in that manner which best declares the historic continuity of the ministry from the age of the Apostles. Our own Bishop Lightfoot's conclusion in his famous Dissertation has certainly not lost validity in the sixty years which have passed since first it was published:

"The threefold ministry can be traced to Apostolic direction and short of an express statement we can possess no better assurance of a Divine appointment or at least a Divine sanction. If the facts do not allow us to unchurch other Christian communities differently organised, they may at least justify our jealous adhesion to a polity derived from this source."

Modern historical science beyond all question authenticates the statement with which the Preface to the English Ordinal opens:

"It is evident unto all men diligently reading holy Scripture and ancient Authours, that from the Apostles' time there have been these Orders of Ministers in Christ's Church; Bishops, Priests, and Deacons."

There is real value in these visible and recognised evidences of the Commission. It is worth much to

stand in a great succession of ordered spiritual
service, to have behind one's efforts the power and
promise of Divine Purpose clearly revealed. Deeper
than any sentimental considerations, stronger than
any formal proofs of validity, is the spiritual assurance that the ministry which you will receive stands
in the line of God's eternal Purpose, is part and
parcel of the mighty movement of redemption which
runs like a Gulf-stream through the centuries, and
was disclosed in its essential meaning in and through
the mission of the Incarnate.

"As the Father sent Me, even so send I you" –
that is the creative utterance of the Divine Lord,
and you will hear it to-morrow in the words which,
in His name and by His authority, I shall speak
when laying on hands at ordination. The knowledge that you are thereby bound into the Divine
Purpose and Policy, and that, as you strive to fulfil
your ministry, you will be passing more and more
consciously and completely into the redemptive
warfare of Jesus Christ, is infinitely consoling and
filled with energising power. "We must work the
works of Him that sent Me while it is day : the night
cometh when no man can work." That is His Word
to us also, linking us with Himself in one and the
same venture. We may be weak : but He is strong.
The knowledge of our weakness, if it throw us
increasingly on His strength, is itself a source of
ministerial power. "His strength is made perfect in

weakness." As His ordained servants we have access to a treasury of spiritual strength which is inexhaustible. Do not doubt that, if you are true to your pledges, He will be true to His promises. You will have your dark hours of failure, or what seems like failure. It may be that to you also will come the deep trouble of doubt and uncertainty, when everything in your self and in your life which is unworthy rises up in mocking challenge, and your heart fails you. But even so you shall not fail. "There is light in the darkness" for loyal hearts. Honest doubt may be the passage to triumphant faith. "Thomas answered and said unto Him, My Lord and my God." Self-abhorrence may lead to a deeper sense of God's sustaining power, as with that prophet whose words I chose as my text. Go forward, then, to your ordination to-morrow with humility and godly fear, but with a sure confidence and a calm mind. "In the world ye shall have tribulation" – runs the Master's Word; and He adds the assurance – "Be of good cheer, I have overcome the world."

V

No man can serve two masters: for either he will hate the one, and love the other: or else he will hold to one, and despise the other. Ye cannot serve God and mammon. Therefore I say unto you, Be not anxious . . .

S. MATTHEW vi. 24, 25

THE SERMON ON THE MOUNT, whether as a whole or in several parts, was addressed to disciples, and not specifically to the Apostles. If I take from it the text on which I propose to base my charge to you on the eve of your ordination, it is because the obligations of discipleship are presupposed and emphasised by appointment to the Christian ministry. It is as men who have openly confessed themselves to be disciples, and on that confession have been accepted by the Church for the work of the ministry, that you will be ordained. For the primary work of the ministry is not merely to proclaim, but to illustrate, the religion of CHRIST. Only as disciples can men be chosen also to become Apostles. The most important pre-requisite for genuine ministry is the hardest to secure, viz. the Christianity of the Christian minister. Very early in her course the *charisma* of "discerning of spirits" was withdrawn from the Church, and she was left to the doubtful evidences of discipleship which her own enquiries and observations could provide. Whatever the Master said of the Christian applies with directer relevance and more solemn emphasis to the Christian minister. Accordingly, I propose that we should read this section of the Sermon, which deals with the single service required from the disciple, as addressed directly to ourselves as men called and commissioned for the ministry.

And, first, let us, in Dr. Johnson's famous phrase, "clear our minds of cant" when we consider the actual situation of the English clergyman in modern society. "Ye cannot serve God and mammon." I shall hope to show you that even in these days, when the Christian ministry has long been reckoned among the professions, there is (or, at least, there ought to be) a sense in which to be ordained is to prefer the service of God to the service of mammon. But, first, I want to get rid of much conventional thinking and speaking about clerical life. The Christian ministry is not properly described as one of the professions by which men earn their living, and, if they are fortunate, make their fortunes. Such a description is prohibited both by the character and purpose of the Christian minister's work, and by the qualifications which it demands. In truth, the Christian ministry has ever presented a strangely paradoxical aspect. Poverty has been its most frequent condition :

and yet its most persistent shadow has been the worship of mammon. From the first this has been so. S. Peter was careful to warn the "presbyters" against "exercising the oversight" of the Flock of God "for filthy lucre." In the Pastoral Epistles the "bishop" and the "deacon" are specifically exhorted to be "not greedy of filthy lucre." It sets one thinking. Even in those early times, when office in the Christian Church was the surest title to the persecutor's notice, the sordid temptation which the emoluments of clerical office provided was too strong for human virtue. The Lord's words to the multitude might have been addressed throughout Christian history to a great section of the clergy: "Ye seek Me, not because ye saw signs but because ye ate of the loaves, and were filled." Indeed, "the loaves and fishes" has come to be the popular description of ecclesiastical preferment. The difficulty of guarding against sordid motives was great then; it is surely greater now.

We need to remind ourselves, since for the most part we are all poor men, that "covetousness" is the shadow and parasite of poverty rather than of wealth. Rich men are tempted to "be high-minded, and to have their hope set on the uncertainty of riches," but the plenitude of their possessions removes from most of them the sordid craving for gain. Poor men are ever haunted by the temptations to envy and coveting. It is indeed true that the

Church has lost much of her former wealth and dignity, yet it is still the case that her ministry retains enough social prestige and official emolument to make it appeal to men's ambition and avarice. Nor is it merely or mainly the few ecclesiastical positions which used to be called the "prizes of the profession" that justify this statement, but the general aspect of the English clergyman's position in the popular regard. Go into one of our mining parishes, even one where the parochial organisation is recent and relatively mean, and note how the vicarage, often pleasantly set in its garden, stands out conspicuously among the squalid houses in which the people live; and how the vicar's income, generally at least £400 per annum, is considerably greater than that of most of his parishioners. There are parishes, generally the old rectories, where the contrast is much sharper, but I am speaking of the general type. It is the fact that the English clergyman is better housed and better paid than the bulk of the people to whom he ministers. You must not be surprised, then, to discover that, while the ecclesiastical world rings with the cry of clerical poverty, it is rather the material comfort of the clergy that most impresses their own parishioners. In these circumstances it would be mere affectation to pretend that there is no need for the apostolic warning against "filthy lucre" in the case of men who in modern England seek ordination to the

Christian ministry. Mostly they are poor men, and there has been little in their upbringing to create large expectations in their minds. It is certain that, as clergymen, they will not be required to accept a lower standard of comfort than that to which they have been accustomed. Why, then, should they be discontented with their lot? Yet discontent is terribly common among English clergymen to-day. I am sure that one of the most potent causes of clerical failure is the discontented spirit which fills so many clergymen's minds, and finds expression on their lips. Too often they compare their lot, not with that of their people, but with the richer lay-folk whom they come to know; and they take it as a personal hardship that they have not the same comforts and pleasures. Yet we are for ever speaking from the pulpit about the duty of contentment, the relative unimportance of secular boons, and the obligation of self-denial. Our private speech too often gives the lie to our public teaching: and thereby we become the architects of our own official failure. Let us settle it with ourselves, here and now, that as clergymen we have been called to suffer hardship "as good soldiers of Jesus Christ"; that, for the most part, we are set to live among poor and hard-working people, and that we can only live there usefully as ourselves also poor and hardworking; that our personal claim begins and ends with sufficient maintenance at our sacred employment; that unless our people can see in us, wherever we may be placed in the hierarchy, a disinterested, unworldly spirit, they will never heed our spiritual message; that we are called to be examples of manly simplicity and self-respecting independence, not of self-pleasing, and easy living, and querulous discontent, and unworthy complaining. Remember the pledge:

"Will you apply all your diligence to frame and fashion your own lives, and the lives of your families, according to the Doctrine of Christ: and to make both yourselves and them, as much as in you lieth, wholesome examples of the flock of Christ?

"I will so do, the Lord being my helper."

You must try honestly to live in obedience to that pledge.

"No man can serve two masters" – οὐδεὶς δύναται δυσὶ κυρίοις δουλεύειν. We must give full force to the significant word – δουλεύειν. A man may well enough work for two employers, for he may covenant with the one for part of his time, and with the other for the remainder. But a man can hardly be the slave of two owners, equally subject to the will of both. "No man can be slave to two owners. Ye cannot be God's slave and also mammon's." For here there is no question of free agreement in service, but of personal status. You are either God's slave, owned by Him, and wholly subject to His will, or you are mammon's slave, mammon's property, and mammon's pledged thrall. So S. Paul speaks of "covetousness," the spirit of mammon's worship, as itself equivalent to a religion. "Covetousness which is idolatry" is his striking phrase.

This ownership by God which is the essence of all discipleship, and which is the openly confessed law of Christian ministry, means much, so much, indeed, that I think we may without extravagance find in it the meaning of that "cross" which He said must be carried by His followers. So incorrigibly social is human nature, that it cries out in protest against any handling of itself which demands a way of life which is in appearance and in general estimate anti-social, unpopular, odd. From the first, this oddity has attached conspicuously to the Christian minister. It was supremely illustrated in the apostolate. "I think," writes S. Paul to the Corinthians, "God hath set forth us the apostles last of all, as men doomed to death: for we are made a spectacle unto the world, and to angels, and to men. We are fools for Christ's sake . . . we are made as the filth of the world, the offscouring of all things, even until now."

No doubt the circumstances in which the Christian ministry has to be fulfilled have greatly changed. The "hard, pagan world" of antiquity, in which the Apostle of the Gentiles ran his glorious course, and gained his martyr's crown, has given place to the Christendom we know, that is, an order of civilised life which, though not truly to be described as

Christian, is yet in aspect, habit, temper, and speech, largely Christianised. The position of the clergy could not remain unaffected by the change of social and political environment. In our country (which in some respects remains the most faithful representative of the medieval polity) the clergy, or spirituality, constitute the first estate of the realm, the archbishop is the first subject not of royal blood, and many of the bishops are peers of Parliament. The ancient dominance of the clergy survives in many social customs, and in a deference, not wholly insincere, which still marks the language of English people. All this is plainly passing, but it has not yet passed, and, while it lasts, it tends to obscure the realities of the clergyman's position.. The sharp distinction between clergy and laity in the ordering of personal life, in the employment of leisure, even in dress, as well as in specific duties, on which the ancient Canon Law insists, and which both the ordination vows and our English canons continue to require, does, if you consider it seriously, constitute a self-subordination of the clergyman to an arbitrary discipline which asks much of him. Take the comparatively unimportant case of the clergyman's dress. The 74th Canon of 1604, headed, "Decencie in apparell enjoyned to Ministers," is, of course, so far as its positive directions go, archaic and practically obsolete, but it states a fact and embodies a principle which we may not rightly or prudently ignore. There has been in recent years a notable recognition of the disciplinary value of uniform especially among the young. Church Lads' Brigade, Boy Scouts, Girl Guides, are all dressed distinctively, and for an excellent reason. The character implied by membership of the organisation, by being thus visibly certified, has been the more effectively accepted. A sense of corporate honour has been created, and an auxiliary to the frail force of personal purpose discovered and brought into play. The time-honoured motive, *Noblesse oblige*, has received a salutary extension, and, without their being conscious of the fact, has determined the behaviour of rough lads and girls. Curiously enough this new recognition of the disciplinary value of uniform among the young has gone along with a notable carelessness about their own official dress among the clergy. While the emphasising of distinctive character is aimed at in the one case, the obliteration of distinctive character would appear to be aimed at in the other. It is quite common now to see clergymen so dressed as to be almost indistinguishable from laymen. It must be the more easy for them to forget their corporate obligation, and to ignore the severe demands of their incommunicable obligation. My deliberate judgment, which you must take for what it is worth, only remembering that it is the judgment of one who has had long experience of the Christian ministry and seen much of its working in varying circumstances, and who is, moreover, your own bishop, I say, my deliberate judgment condemns this new laxity in the matter of clerical dress. I think it lowers the clergyman's standard of personal obligation, and tends to sink the layman's estimate of the clergyman's ministry. For myself, I do not find the language of the 74th Canon archaic or irrelevant:

"The true, ancient and flourishing Churches of Christ being ever desirous that their Prelacie and Cleargie might be had as well in outward reverence, as otherwise regarded for the worthinesse of their Ministry, did think it fit by a prescript forme of decent and comely Apparell, to have them knowen to the people, and thereby to receive the honor and estimation due to the special Messengers and Ministers of Almighty God. Wee therefore following their grave judgement, and the ancient Custome of the Church of England, and hoping that in time new fanglenesse of Apparell in some factious persons will die of itself, do constitute and appoint."

There is a familiar, decorous, and convenient mode of clerical dress generally used by English clergymen. I must needs think that it argues either frivolity or conceit to exchange it for something different. I hope that none of you will do this. It surely needs not that I should tell you that this rule about dress must be obeyed intelligently. It does not apply to games in which a clergyman may rightly and usefully join, and which require a suitable dress. Nor does it disallow the adoption of holiday garb,

provided always that the clerical character is not
concealed. The clergyman is never in such sense off
duty as to be free to disguise himself. But the rule
does properly apply to the clergyman's life in the
parish. There his proper and professed character
ought to be apparent.

Take the more important matter of the clergyman's reading. Not only is the point emphasised in
the long exhortation which forms so prominent and
impressive a feature of the ordering of priests, but
it forms the substance of one of the ordination vows:

"Will you be diligent in Prayers, and in reading of
the holy Scriptures, and in such studies as help to the
knowledge of the same, laying aside the study of the
world and the flesh?

"I will endeavour myself so to do, the Lord being my
helper."

The exhortation was the composition of the
Huguenot divine, Martin Bucer, and it reflects the
somewhat lop-sided conception of the Christian
minister's function which the vehement reaction
against medieval sacerdotalism did unquestionably
occasion. Moreover, it has evident relation to social
and intellectual conditions which have largely passed
away. It is, therefore, fairly, nay inevitably, subjected to a considerable discount, when it is applied
to the guidance of modern clergymen. But, even so,
it states with solemnity and a moving urgency truths

about the Christian minister's obligation which we dare not belittle or neglect. If we must admit that it illustrates that pathetic confidence in the spiritual value of exhortation which marked the Reformers, and has added a distinctive feature to the English formularies, we must also admit that it emphasises aspects of the priest's duty which the circumstances of our time make it particularly easy for him to underrate or even wholly to ignore. Besides, we must give some coherent and adequate meaning to the ordination vow which we are about to take. What do we mean by the rather formidable phrase, "laying aside the study of the world and the flesh"? Clearly, the clergyman's reading must be determined by motives which will not determine the layman's.

Two distinct, but closely allied, considerations will govern the one, and not the other: (1) the faithful exercise of the clergyman's function as a religious teacher, and (2) the requirements of his own personal efficiency for all the purposes of his ministry. The first controls his professional studies; the last determines his general reading. I need not remind you that the expounding of the Holy Scriptures, which is the normal duty of the parish clergyman, requires a far larger range of knowledge now than was formerly requisite. Some acquaintance with history, criticism, and psychology is indispensable, as well as familiarity with the sacred text and an adequate grasp of theology. Mere exhortation is so common now, and is so freely given by untrained laymen, that a special importance has come to belong to the preaching of the clergy. It ought to be so plainly related to trained thinking and relevant knowledge, that the congregations will be under no temptation to regard it as essentially identical with, and nowise more important than, the pious outpourings of laymen. When, however, we pass from the studies which are concerned directly with the exposition of the Scripture, to the general or miscellaneous reading which affects our personal efficiency, we find ourselves confronted by a host of difficulties. Not only is the range of choice practically unlimited, but the specific requirements of every man will vary with his temperament, situation, and culture. The newspapers, the novels, the biographies, the general histories, the technical or semi-technical books of all the sciences, the speculative treatises which pass as philosophical, all the mingled mass of current literature – what place may any, or all of these books have in a faithful clergyman's life?

You must be your own spiritual director. Nobody else knows, or can be made to know, enough about you for that office.

The *Index Expurgatorius*, which shall limit your reading of novels, must be that which your own conscience frames. None can take over the responsibility which is incommunicably yours. I counsel you to keep your mind fresh by some intellectual pursuit, lying apart from, but not incongruous with, your professional studies, which interests you, and which may become in your hands valuable, not only as assisting your personal efficiency, but also as providing an approach to some of your people. A healthy hobby is a valuable possession for every man, and especially for every parish clergyman. Don't waste too much time on the newspapers, and never attach much importance to anything they may say about you or your work. If they denounce you for your faults, think how much more effectively they could do it if they really knew the entire truth. If they applaud you, which is the more general method of insult, remember how little right they have to sit in judgment on your work.

"The Lord's servant must not strive," says the Apostle. I think that his words have directest reference to the eager resentment of personal affronts which is so natural to us all, and, perhaps, never so easy as when it can be disguised as something more respectable.

I must make an end of my charge, and it must be on the notes of comfort and encouragement, not on those of warning and counsel. For truly the notes of comfort and encouragement are most audible in the Master's words, uncompromising and decisive though they are, when they are heard by those who, with sincere and resolute purpose, are offering themselves for ordination to the ministry. If, and surely this is the case with us, we have taken our side deliberately, and with open eyes have accepted the ownership of God in discipleship, frankly surrendering ourselves – body, mind, and spirit – in willing obedience to His will, then we are set free from every other bondage, and brought into possession of that "perfect freedom" which His service, and His service alone, can give to the children of men. "Therefore," because you are indeed "God's slaves," "I say unto you, Be not anxious." "Never forget that you are the servant of Another," said the late Bishop of Liverpool, Dr. Chavasse, to me once, when I was more than commonly perplexed and depressed by the untoward aspect of ecclesiastical affairs, in which the way of my personal duty seemed to be completely obscured. His words, so simple and indeed so obvious, carried to my mind a message of genuine consolation. "The servant of Another," not responsible therefore for the Message with its enormous difficulty, "The stumblingblock of the cross," nor yet for the besieging embarrassments of my actual ministry, but only for my personal loyalty to Him, the Divine Lord, whom I am pledged to serve, and whose will it is that I should serve Him here and now. "The servant of Another," "God's slave," that character calls for humility, and withal carries the assurance of strength. Were not the Master's words in the text running in S. Peter's mind when he penned his admonition to the presbyters, with which I will bring my charge to an end:

"Humble yourselves therefore under the mighty hand of God, that He may exalt you in due time: casting all your anxiety upon Him, because He careth for you."

VI

Suffer hardship with me, as a good soldier of Christ Jesus. No soldier on service entangleth himself in the affairs of this life: that he may please him who enrolled him as a soldier. And if also a man contend in the games, he is not crowned except he have contended lawfully.

2 TIMOTHY ii. 3–5

ON THE EVE OF YOUR ORDINATION, I desire to speak to you frankly about the claims and conditions of the new life into which ordination will introduce you. It is, of course, true that the diaconate which you will receive to-morrow is an "inferior office," and that only when you receive the priesthood will you have received the full commission to the Christian ministry. Still, it is the settled practice of the Church of England to treat the diaconate as no more than a brief apprenticeship to the priesthood, so that the decisive step out of the secular into the ecclesiastical life will have been taken when you have received ordination to the diaconate. Short of some incapacitating circumstance, I shall look forward to the privilege of ordaining you to the priesthood next year. Accordingly, I shall speak to-night on the

assumption that you are about to enter on the life
and work of Christian ministers.

"Life and Work" – that is the natural, but, alas!
not the invariable order. First, the Christian life:
next, the Christian minister's commission. Until we
have heard and obeyed the vocation to the Christian
discipleship, we cannot claim to have received the
vocation to the apostolic ministry. In the Church
Christ acts still as He acted at the first when, in the
persons of the Twelve Apostles, He instituted the
ministry which is perpetuated by ordination. He
selects out of the disciples those who shall be Apostles.
So S. Luke writes: "When it was day, He called His
disciples: and He chose from them twelve." It
cannot be superfluous to remind you of what might
seem too obvious to need statement. For it is disastrously possible for men to be nominally ministers of
Christ, and even for them to work as such with great
apparent success, and to draw to themselves a large
popularity thereby, who yet have never been truly
His disciples, and are surely destined to be repu-
diated by Him at the last. There is, to my thinking,
no more terrifying utterance in the whole gospel than
that severe warning in the Sermon on the Mount:
"Many will say to Me in that day, Lord, Lord, did
we not prophesy by Thy name, and by Thy name
cast out devils, and by Thy name do many mighty
works. And then will I profess unto them, I never
knew you: depart from Me ye that work iniquity."

The temptation to seek the ministry for unworthy reasons was strangely strong even in that early age when, we might have thought, the inducements to hypocrisy were small. To be a Christian then was to come under the frown of society, and, perhaps, to be brought into collision with the public authorities. To be a Christian minister was to be set in the front of the battle. Yet we have but to read the Apostolic Epistles to learn that the vices of ambition, covetousness, and a mechanical professionalism were even then bringing shame on the ministry. Consider the implications of S. Peter's admonition to the presbyters: "Tend the flock of God which is among you, exercising the oversight, not of constraint, but willingly, according unto God; nor yet for filthy lucre, but of a ready mind; neither as lording it over the charge allotted to you, but making yourselves ensamples to the flock." Formalism, greed, arrogance are all clearly indicated in these earnest and moving words. In our own age assuredly the danger is not less, though it has largely changed its form. The Church of Christ has long been established in England, and for centuries the clergy have formed the first estate of the realm. The Christian ministry is reckoned among the professions by which men earn their livings, and it has its professional rules, standards, and remuneration. It is, then, very easy for us to forget that, though the ministry is a profession, yet it must always be something greater. Inevitably

E

the combination of a profession and a spiritual
service leads to much confusion of thought and
speech, and makes terribly easy a vast amount of
sophistical casuistry and unconscious hypocrisy.
Perhaps, however, there is less spiritual danger in the
professionalising of spiritual office (though truly this
is very great) than in the stimulus to self-delusion
which comes from the conditions under which
clerical life proceeds in a modern democracy. Excessive publicity for the clergyman goes along with a
very slight and shallow acquaintance with the man
himself. Grand reputations may be gained very
cheaply. Whatever in his performance of duty is
picturesque, abnormal, or dramatic will command
excessive advertisement: whatever is quiet, steady,
self-sacrificing, spiritual, will be ignored or mis-
represented. The local reporters assist with their
flattering superlatives the vanity which is rarely
lacking, and a large popularity in the district may go
along with a strangely small amount of genuine
work and with even less genuine devotion. We may
all of us take to heart that censure which our Master
passed on the Pharisees: "They loved the glory of
men more than the glory of God." I need not dwell
longer on these things. Remember when men speak
or write well of you, how very little they can really
know. Set beside their compliments what you
yourself know about your own personal record and
habit: and bethink you of the judgment of Him who

knows the whole truth about you, and cannot be hoodwinked by the claptrap of newspapers and the interested approbation of partisans. Let the lowly prayer of the psalmist be often on your lips – never so often as in the days when "all men speak well of you" – "Who can tell how oft he offendeth: O cleanse thou me from my secret faults. Keep thy servant also from presumptuous sins, lest they get the dominion over me: so shall I be undefiled, and innocent from the great offence. Let the words of my mouth, and the meditation of my heart: be alway acceptable in thy sight, O Lord my strength and my redeemer."

The life of the clergyman is none other than the life of a Christian man, publicly certified to be such, and certified by his own deliberate request. There cannot be two standards of right living in the Christian family, but there is an almost infinite variety of circumstances, and for every Christian, layman as well as clergyman, his personal obligation must be determined with reference to his actual situation. Every position carries a specific require-ment: every relation brings a specific demand. The "mind of Christ" has to be disclosed under varying conditions. Public opinion has its claims, and indi-vidual weakness, and particular opportunities, and private needs. "Take thought for things honourable in the sight of all men," writes the Apostle. "We take thought for things honourable, not only in the

sight of the Lord, but also in the sight of men."
S. Paul is the greatest model of pastorate that the
Church possesses, and he is also the first great
Christian casuist. He has drawn his own picture, and
it is a picture of almost limitless self-subordination
to the limitations of others' weakness, prejudice, and
ignorance. "I am become all things to all men, that
I may by all means save some." He is saved from an
immoral complaisance, which might too easily grow
from such a habit of self-surrender for the gospel's
sake, by his intense consciousness of duty to his
Divine Master. "We preach not ourselves, but
Christ Jesus as Lord, and ourselves as your servants
for Jesus' sake." His complaisance is thus conditioned by a rigorous loyalty to Christian principles.
"Prove all things," he says; and adds immediately,
"Hold fast that which is good: abstain from every
form of evil."

The clergyman's private life has an evident bearing
on his personal influence, which indeed it may be
said to determine. Now this is of even greater
importance than may at first sight appear, for the
clergyman's personal influence is being fashioned,
surely and silently, by his daily life, and has comparatively little relation to the deliberate exercise of
his ministry; and that personal influence, of which
perhaps he is hardly conscious, is his main weapon
for the spiritual conflict to which he is Divinely
commissioned. For in truth all his conscious and

formal efforts will be affected by it. Who will listen to a man whom one does not respect? And who will respect a man who is seen to fall below the standards of conduct which he officially affirms? Who will turn for counsel to a man whom one has ground for thinking stands in greater need of good counsel even than one's own self? Remember that your parishioners will judge you primarily in those common experiences with which they are familiar. Here it is that the careful, even scrupulous, fulfilment of ordinary social duties becomes in the clergyman's case so important. "Making both ends meet" is a difficult problem for many of the clergy, but they must remember that nothing else is the task which thousands of laity, even poorer than themselves, have to face. If, then, the clergyman should fall into debt, he will assuredly fall into moral discredit. He will have been put to the common test, and failed to sustain it. If the clergyman be a married man, there are all the difficulties of family life to be reckoned with. But these also are part and parcel of the common burden. If the layman see his clergyman's family ill-disciplined, the clergyman's house ill-managed, the clergyman's garden ill-kept, how is it anywise to be expected that he will respect the clergyman himself, or heed his counsels? It is not the poverty of the clergy which ruins their influence, but their evident inability to solve the practical problems which poverty presents not only to the clergy, but to the main multitude of the laity. "Set not your minds on high things," says S. Paul, "but condescend to things that are lowly."

You will be "appointed to preach," and then the spiritual effectiveness of your preaching will be determined, to an extent which it is difficult to exaggerate, by your personal character and reputation. Instinctively the people will discern how far your words answer to your beliefs. The preacher stands before his congregation as "the ambassador of Christ." His words, therefore, must have behind them the motive of personal conviction, and the authority of personal experience. Only on that supposition will the consciences of honest men tolerate his claim to speak with authority in the name of Christ. The notion of a merely forensic advocacy of the gospel, such as the barrister brings to the service of his client, is wholly intolerable. No contradiction can be imagined more repulsive and degrading than that which is presented by the spectacle of an unbelieving preacher. The mere suspicion of personal insincerity is enough to destroy the preacher's influence, and to sterilise his ministry.

"A traitorous commander, that shooteth nothing against the enemy but powder, may cause his guns to make as great a sound or report as some that are laden with bullets: but he doth no hurt to the enemy by it. So one of these men may speak loud, and mouth it with an affected fervency: but he seldom doth any great execution against sin and Satan."

Thus quaintly does Richard Baxter describe the spiritual futility of a ministry which is vitiated at the root by a lack of conviction.

You will often have to lead the worship of the congregation by reading the appointed prayers and lessons. It will be but too easy for you to become careless and even irreverent unless you are on your guard. There can be no reasonable question that non-Anglicans who attend our services do but too often receive an impression of formalism which may even suggest an apparent insincerity. I hesitate to offer you any specific advice with respect to the manner of your reading and preaching in church, because the attempt to follow it might go far towards defeating my object. Naturalness is of the essence of good reading. It is related of Archbishop Whately, an outspoken man who had small patience with anything canting and pretentious, that he was urged by a clergyman to give his opinion as to the manner in which the said clergyman read the service. He answered brusquely:

" 'Well, then, if you really wish to know what I think of your reading, I should say that there are only two parts of the service you read well, and those you read unexceptionably.' – 'And what are these?' said the clergyman. 'They are, "Here endeth the first lesson," and "Here endeth the second lesson." ' 'What do you mean, Whately?' 'I mean,' he replied, 'that those parts you read in your own natural voice and manner, which are very good: the rest is all artificial and assumed.' "[1]

This criticism was both acute and just. Even if you have to exert yourself in speaking in order to be heard clearly, as is commonly the case in large buildings, and even when you have to manage your voice with deliberate care, as is always the case in Gothic cathedrals, you need not be unnatural. What men speak of disgustedly as a "pulpit voice" is the final triumph of art, debased art, over nature. Any suggestion of self-consciousness, or artificiality, or deliberate effort to produce an effect is fatal to devotion, distracts the attention of the people, and may even be offensive. George Herbert's chapter on "The Parson's Praying" reflects the habit of the XVIIth century, and would not be relevant to that of our own time. His actual counsel as to the clergyman's attitude and gestures may be safely disregarded, but he goes to the root of the matter when he connects the parson's performance of his duty in church with his state of mind and religious habit. A worthy rendering of the public service is still conditioned by these:

"This he doth, first, as being truly touched and amazed with the Majesty of God before whom he then presents himself: yet not as himself alone, but as presenting with himself the whole Congregation, whose sins he

[1] v. *Life*, p. 46.

then bears and brings with his own to the heavenly altar
to be bathed and washed in the sacred Laver of Christ's
Blood. Secondly, as this is the true reason of his inward
fear, so he is content to express this outwardly to the
utmost of his power; that being first affected himself,
he may affect also his people, knowing that no Sermon
moves them so much to a reverence, which they forget
again when they come to pray, as a devout behaviour
in the very act of praying."

Do not allow yourselves to speak lightly or even
disrespectfully of Mattins and Evensong, as if by so
doing you would the more effectually exalt the Holy
Eucharist. Our Church, in that "Prayer of S.
Chrysostom" which concludes both Mattins and
Evensong, pleads the Saviour's promise of His
presence and answer to His people's prayer "when
two or three are gathered together in His Name."
It is a medieval superstition which would limit the
Lord's presence to the Blessed Sacrament, though
we must needs believe that therein that presence is
most richly manifested for the sustenance of His
people. The familiar hymn, which is sung in our
churches, does but paraphrase the very words of the
Redeemer:

> Jesus, where'er Thy people meet,
> There they behold Thy mercy-seat:
> Where'er they seek Thee Thou art found,
> And every place is hallow'd ground.

The best security for a reverent regard for the
Holy Eucharist is the habit of true reverence for

E*

God's service as a whole. If the clergyman lets the people see, by his flippant speech and careless manner, that he holds the other services of the Sanctuary in light esteem, let him know of a surety that he is breaking down reverence in their minds, and leading them to an unworthy view even of the Blessed Sacrament itself.

Let me pause for one moment on a matter which may seem unimportant, but yet carries no small issues. The shortage of clergy has, among many other baleful consequences, the effect of often compelling the clergy to take many services. They hasten from one place to another in motors and on motor-cycles, arriving hurried and heated, sometimes with mud-bespattered clothes and defiled hands, on the very stroke of the hour, in order to celebrate the Divine Mysteries. In such circumstances it needs a very resolute sense of duty and a genuine personal devotion if the clergyman is to maintain a worthy standard of personal reverence and decency. Take thought for this danger, and, so far as you can, be on your guard against it. It is a real danger, and the level of congregational devotion is, unless I gravely misread the facts, being lowered by it. The same cause, shortage of clergy, compels the employment of laymen to do what is truly the clergyman's work. Now the laymen are frequently honest and sincere persons, of rough habits and uncultivated speech. Their ministrations, which are in the actual

circumstances of the Church indispensable, may
well habituate the congregations to a lower level of
public worship and teaching than is edifying. It
follows that a special responsibility rests on the
ordained clergy to be very watchful against anything in their own performance of duty which can
tend to encourage an irreverent habit.

You are entering on your sacred employment at
a time of grave, perhaps unprecedented, difficulty;
and you will probably be required to accept the full
pastoral responsibility as incumbents of parishes very
soon – far sooner than has been general in the past.
Unless you show yourselves plainly incompetent
for independent charge, or some incapacitating
circumstance of which we as yet know nothing
shall emerge, you will be appointed in a very few
years to be incumbents of parishes. Take care, then,
that you are modest, teachable, and laborious. Let
these few precious years of training be so used that
when the time comes you will not be wholly unequal
to the larger duty proposed to you. Look carefully
after your personal religion. None can look after that
save yourself: and yet it is the fact which determines
everything else. Be watchful against the sins of the
flesh – sloth, self-indulgence, impurity. Exercise
yourselves in all things that make for righteousness.
It is a hard labour that lies before you, a difficult
quest, but the reward of perseverance is great.
Listen to the humble and agonistic words of the

Apostle, and adopt them as the formula of your own ministry: "Know ye not that they which run in a race run all, but one receiveth the prize? Even so run, that ye may attain. And every man that striveth in the games is temperate in all things. Now they do it to receive a corruptible crown; but we an incorruptible. I therefore so run, as not uncertainly; so fight I, as not beating the air: but I buffet my body, and bring it into bondage: lest by any means, after that I have preached to others, I myself should be rejected."

VII

EVERY HUMAN EMPLOYMENT HAS, at least, two aspects
– individual and social. It expresses the man; and
it affects the community of which he is a member.
However self-centred and socially aloof a man may
be, he cannot escape contact with his fellows, coming
under their influence, and bringing them under his.
"No man liveth to himself; and none dieth to himself." "We are members one of another." Shakespeare states the truth in his own grand manner,
when he writes:

> "Thy self and thy belongings
> Are not thine own so proper, as to waste
> Thyself upon thy virtues, they on thee.
> Heaven doth with us as we with torches do,
> Not light them for themselves; for if our virtues
> Did not go forth of us, 'twere all alike
> As if we had them not. Spirits are not finely touch'd
> But to fine issues——"[1]

That the possession of gifts and privileges is itself
a vocation to their unselfish use, and to such a use as

---

[1] v. *Measure for Measure*, Act I., sc. i.

is congruous with their excellence, is a deeply suggestive thought, entirely accordant with the Christian conception of duty. And yet, while thus we are closely knit into society, we are always individuals, inexorably distinctive and alone. "No man may deliver his brother, nor make agreement unto God for him." "To his own master he standeth or falleth." Our rigorous loyalty to the claims of self is the pledge and condition of our frank fulfilment of social duty. "Thou shalt love thy neighbour as thyself" is the royal law. The Christian ministry, then, must be considered from these two points of view: What does it mean for the man who is charged with it? What does it mean for the Church, in which and for which it exists?

On the eve of your ordination, it is fitting, and ought to be useful, to think over both these questions, and, perhaps, especially over the first.

Ordination means for the man who receives it sincerely, at least these three things:

(1) The beginning of his professional career.

(2) The public and deliberate profession of Christianity.

(3) The response to a Divine vocation affirmed in, and owned by, the Church of Christ.

Look more closely at these implications of your ordination.

I. THE CHRISTIAN MINISTRY AS A PROFESSION

In our country, where the Christian religion has been officially recognised for more than twelve centuries, and where the Church is still legally established, the ministry ranks as one of the professions by which men earn their living. It is traditionally the first in dignity of the learned professions. The law still invests it with a high prestige. In Burke's famous phrase, the Church of England "rears its mitred front in Courts and Parliaments," though these have lost much of their former importance. Professional motives, then, can hardly be excluded from the process by which men reach the decision to become clergymen, and these may be neither exalted nor trustworthy. Ambition and even cupidity may find their way under respectable disguises into the young man's mind. While, for obvious reasons, the clergyman is excluded from secular employments, and may not "make money" by his ministry, he is paid an income which, though never very large, is not often very small. In theory, and generally in fact, the clergyman's income is secure and sufficient. He is, as men say, "maintained at his job," and if he be reasonably efficient, and bear a good character, that "job" will never be lacking. After a brief apprenticeship as an assistant curate, he will normally be appointed to a "benefice," and possess what is commonly called a "living." Let me remind you that the first duty of the clergyman, as of every other good citizen, is to *earn* his living. To do this will be, perhaps, in his case considerably more difficult than in the case of other professional men. For his living, unlike theirs, is secured to him whether he earn it or not. Not only is efficiency largely unconditioned by remuneration in the clergyman's case, but, also, the nature of the clergyman's work makes the determining of efficiency extremely difficult. The ordinary tests of professional efficiency rarely apply to him. No balance sheet duly certified can prove his soundness; no popular applause is worth anything as an evidence of his fulfilment of duty; no professional success can be safely regarded as a proof of spiritual quality. The ordinary guarantees of efficiency are largely absent from the clergyman's life. There is no professional man so largely left to himself in the matter of ordering and measuring his exertions as the clergyman. His legal obligations are neither numerous nor exacting. His manner of performing them may involve very petty exertions, whether of mind or body. So far as his official, prescribed, and legally enforceable work is concerned, the clergyman's work must be considered easy. In the phrase of the market-place, he "has a light job."

Yet the essential conditions of professional efficiency are not different for the clergyman than for all other professional men. Not less than the doctor, the lawyer, and the schoolmaster, the clergyman must be adequately educated; must acquire by experience that practical knowledge which nothing but experience can provide; must win such a measure of public confidence as shall induce men to accept his professional service; must know and observe the discipline of his profession; must avoid carefully what is regarded as "unprofessional conduct." If it may be urged, that, in the case of all other professions, the reward of professional efficiency is expressed in a waxing professional income, it may be pointed out that only in the clergyman's case is a "living wage" secured from the first, and employment normally guaranteed. I dwell on these matters because I desire to warn you against that querulous discontented temper which is too common among the clergy, and which does undoubtedly facilitate that mendicant habit which brings discredit on the whole ministry.

Remember, as your first professional obligation, to make yourselves efficient. I will but instance three particulars to which your attention should be directed.

(1) *Be sure that you know the law and custom of your profession.* When, in a few years' time, you become incumbents, you will be responsible for the practical application of many statutes. You should make a point of acquainting yourselves with the laws which govern the parish priest with respect to the conduct

of divine service in the parish church, the celebration of marriages, the control of the churchyard, the parochial schools and charities, and many other matters. Ignorance of law leads sometimes to very serious consequences.

Ecclesiastical law is changing very rapidly. Whatever may be thought of the quality of the legislation which, under the provisions of the Enabling Act, the National Assembly has carried, there can be no two opinions about its quantity. To the knowledge of the law, I have added that of the custom of the profession. You should avoid pedantry and mere individualism. "Use and wont" is the rightful authority over a great part of professional duty. To do the right thing in a novel, and, therefore, unpleasing and suspected manner, is hardly less mischievous than doing the wrong thing. The Apostolic injunctions to "take thought for things honourable in the sight of all men," and "not to let your good be evil spoken of" have a direct and important bearing on your manner of obeying the law.

(2) *Try to acquire a sound professional habit.* There is a middle way of established procedure which avoids clerical affectation, on the one hand, and an aggressive mimicry of laymanship on the other. In every profession there is a tradition of conduct which it is unwise to ignore, and dangerous to condemn. The layman's dislike of the clergyman's indulgence in modes of language and behaviour, which he thinks

venial in his own case, has perhaps more respectable roots than we always allow. It is right and reasonable that he should expect self-control, gravity, a certain reverence of speech and manner in the man who is the ordained minister of Christ. On the golf course, or on the football field, in the club, and the smoking-room, in the hotel, and on shipboard during the annual holiday, the clergyman is still "on duty," and he should be watchful against forgetfulness of the fact. Within recent years, especially since the War, there has been a general laying aside of those pro-fessional distinctions which a former generation, perhaps, tended to over-emphasise, and this change of social habit has certainly facilitated a perilous secularisation of the clergy. In these circumstances, I must needs think that there is real need for vigilance. "I speak as to wise men: judge ye what I say."

(3) *Study your human material*. Here the special value of pastoral visitation appears to my mind most apparent. Of all pastoral methods this, in my deliberate judgment, based on the experience and observation of a long ministry, remains the most valuable. Its effect is not only to be found in the attitude of the parishioners, but in the understanding of the parish clergyman. Thereby he is enabled to discern and to appreciate the wealth of individuality which even a small parish presents. In S. John's picture of the Good Shepherd, this individualising treatment of the flock is emphasised. "He calleth

His own sheep by name and leadeth them out."
This action of the Good Shepherd calls forth in the
"sheep" an answering devotion, deep and dis-
criminating. "A stranger will they not follow, but
will flee from him: for they know not the voice of
strangers." Tact is an indispensable element in the
parish priest's efficiency, not the cowardly calculation
which simply seeks to avoid giving offence, when,
perhaps, offence is the very thing which ought to
be given, but the charitable consideration which is
anxious to make sure that no avoidable hindrance
is placed in the way, and no unnecessary misunderstanding occasioned. We clergy are really in a
true sense artists, and it is indispensable that we
should understand the material with which, as
artists, we have to work. That material is human
nature, incorrigibly individual, amazingly various
in condition and circumstance, strangely perverted,
prejudiced, and sensitively proud, yet full of latent
goodness, and always capable of quite astonishing
moral recoveries. One of the main sources of
pastoral inefficiency in the English clergy to-day is
their ignorance of their own people, an ignorance
born partly of the neglect of pastoral visitation, but
partly caused by the very brief tenure of parochial
charge which now marks the Church of England.
Knowledge of individual idiosyncrasy cannot be
improvised; it must be slowly garnered from
personal intercourse.

II. The Christian Ministry as the Public and Deliberate Profession of Christianity

Do we, who bear the commission of the Christian ministry, remember sufficiently that it implies for us the public and sustained profession of the Christian discipleship? For us, alone of all the types of professional men, the distinction between the official life and the personal private life has no validity. If it be the case that there are not two standards of morality, the one for the clergyman, and the other for the layman, it is not the less the case (and, perhaps, this is the more important truth so far as the clergyman is concerned) that the clergyman alone comes into society avowing himself to be a Christian, and claiming from his fellows that they should so regard, appraise, and judge him. So important is this fact that it is emphasised at ordination, when the deacon and the priest are required to pledge themselves to live Christianly. It might, indeed, have been supposed that this obligation was so plain and evident that it might fairly be assumed. How could the Christian minister ever forget that he was always and everywhere a Christian man? But the Church knows too well that "familiarity breeds contempt," that the very circumstances in which the clergyman lives may render him indifferent to his private duty, and that his official emphasis on the theory of spiritual living may subtly blind him to its practical meaning. Our own Bishop Butler writes in terms of grave warning on this point:

"But going over the theory of virtue in one's thought, talking well, and drawing fine pictures of it; this is so far from necessarily or certainly conducing to form a habit of it, in him who thus employs himself, that it may harden the mind in a contrary course, and render it gradually more insensible, i.e. form a habit of insensibility, to all moral considerations."[1]

Therefore the question at ordination is emphatic, explicit, and inclusive:

"Will you apply all your diligence to frame and fashion your own lives, and the lives of your families, according to the doctrine of Christ; and to make both yourselves and them, as much as in you lieth, wholesome examples to the flock of Christ?

"I will so do, the Lord being my helper."

Sometimes we are disposed to resent, even bitterly, the explicitness of this version of our official duty. We would like to be as little compelled to hold together our public service and our private life as seem to be our lay contemporaries. We would protest with the poet Churchill, himself a clergyman:

"Ah! what, my Lord, hath private life to do
With things of public nature? why to view
Would you thus cruelly those scenes unfold
Which, without pain and horror to behold,

[1] v. *Analogy*, Part I, chap. v.

Must speak me something more, or less than man;
Which friends may pardon, but I never can?
Look back! a thought which borders on despair,
Which human nature must, yet cannot bear.
'Tis not the babbling of a busy world,
Where praise and censure are at random hurl'd,
Which can the meanest of my thoughts control,
Or shake one settled purpose of my soul;
Free and at large might their wild curses roam,
If all, if all, alas! were well at home."

What business is it of any outsider how the clergyman orders his own home, how he employs his
leisure, how he carries himself in all those experiences which lie outside his professional obligation?
That protest is as natural as it is ill-founded. For
ordination not only commissions a minister, but
also certifies a Christian. Henceforward, the
ordained man is the exponent before his fellows of
that theory of life which officially he is appointed
to inculcate. He provides the practical illustration
of his doctrine. His example interprets his precept.
Apart from a congruous personal life, the clergyman's ministry will be spiritually powerless. In the
Sermon on the Mount Christ unites, in his picture
of the rejected minister, great and successful professional activity and lack of personal goodness. The
history of the Church, from the Apostolic Age even
to the present time, has demonstrated the facility and
the frequency of this strange contradiction. The day

of final reckoning will be a day of woeful disillusionment: "Many will say to Me in that day, Lord, Lord, did we not prophesy by Thy name, and by Thy name cast out devils, and by Thy name do many mighty works? And then will I profess unto them, I never knew you: depart from Me ye that work iniquity."

In this connection, the special character of the clergyman's marriage can hardly be omitted. In the Apostolic Age, when the gospel was preached in a world which was apparently and aggressively non-Christian, the union of a believer with a pagan was clearly seen to be irrational, incongruous, and unedifying. The Pauline Rule was both clear and convincing: "Be ye not unequally yoked with unbelievers: for what fellowship have unrighteousness and iniquity? or, what communion hath light with darkness? And what concord hath Christ with Belial? or what portion hath a believer with an unbeliever?" In our modern world, this challenge is again becoming directly relevant to the circumstances in which Christians must consider the question of marriage. To the marriage of clergymen its relevance is most apparent. The XXXIInd Article affirms the clergyman's liberty to marry, but it indicates also the condition under which alone he may rightly exercise that liberty:

"Bishops, Priests, and Deacons, are not commanded by God's Law, either to vow the estate of single life, or to abstain from marriage: therefore it is lawful also for them, as for all other Christian men, to marry at their own discretion, as they shall judge the same to serve better to godliness."

I know no condition more unfavourable to Christian ministry, and certainly none more hostile to personal happiness, than that of an incongruous, unsuitable marriage. And, conversely, there is nothing which more strengthens the clergyman in his sacred task than union with a Christian wife, who enters frankly into his spiritual venture, and helps him to make his home a lesson-book of virtue, discipline, and love to the whole parish.

III. ORDINATION AS THE RESPONSE TO A DIVINE VOCATION, AND THE GIFT OF A DIVINE COMMISSION

When all is said, this cannot but be the paramount thought in your minds to-morrow. You are, as the prophet to whom the Divine Call came wondrously in the Temple: "I heard the Voice of the Lord, saying, Whom shall I send, and who will go for us? Then I said, Here am I : send me. And He said, Go." First of all the solemn and searching questions which the bishop addresses to the young men whom he intends to ordain is the most solemn and the most searching :

"Do you trust that you are inwardly moved by the Holy Ghost to take upon you this office and ministration, to serve God for the promoting of His glory, and the edifying of His people?
"I trust so."

Everything turns on the sincerity with which that answer is made. Apart from the consciousness of Divine commission, what can our ministry mean? Here the Church is helpless: no power to read men's hearts belongs to her. The commission of the ministry it is within her power to give. Authority for its exercise she can bestow. But for the genuineness of the vocation which ordination assumes she cannot vouch. That is the secret which is known only to the candidate himself, and to God, who knows all. I should suppose that there are very few men who would deliberately seek Holy Orders without placing some serious meaning on this primary condition. They must have found some interpretation of the bishop's question which seems to them sufficient to justify their making the requisite answer. Yet the history of the Christian ministry demonstrates that many, very many, of the ordained clergy have never realised what is bound up in that answer. Perhaps we may distinguish the elements which must, on the lowest estimate, combine in a Divine vocation, as it is recognisable here and now. I will name but three:

(1) *Sincere and sustained desire to be ordained.* The suggestion that you should become a clergyman may have arisen in your own heart, you know not when or how; or been brought home to your conscience by some occurrence. The desire arose in your mind, and it persisted. At first, perhaps, it was not altogether welcome, or your circumstances were such that it

seemed altogether irrational. But it persisted. You could not get rid of it, and here, at last, after years of difficulty, which have brought it under a severe testing, it is in your heart, and on your lips. You feel sure that the clergyman's life is the only kind of life for you. None other will satisfy your heart's desire. In none other will you be able to fulfil yourself in service. That conviction must clearly be the primary constituent of a sincere profession of vocation to the ministry.

(2) *Congruity of life and thought.* I have already pointed out that ordination is the public and deliberate profession of Christianity. No man could say honestly that God had called him to become a minister of the gospel, if he habitually violated the morality which the gospel demands, and had no real belief in the truths which the gospel contains. Here the Church herself must accept a large measure of responsibility, but not so large as to exempt the man himself from a grave obligation. In the very forefront of the ordination the requisites of congruous behaviour and belief are emphasised, and a solemn challenge is addressed to the congregation of Christian people present at the ordination.

Let me remind you of that challenge, for, on the eve of your ordination, you should weigh it well:

"Brethren, if there be any of you who knoweth any impediment, or notable crime, in any of these persons presented to be ordered Deacons, for the which he ought not to be admitted to that Office, let him come forth in the Name of God, and show what the crime or impediment is."

That challenge, perhaps, has little practical value; but it deserves our careful thought none the less, because it enshrines a principle of the utmost importance. No man ought to be ordained who is known to be, or who knows himself to be, morally incapacitated. The worst faults are not always the most apparent. A man may bear an excellent reputation among his neighbours who yet knows *that* of himself which, if they were ware of it, would lead them to rise in response to the bishop's challenge and protest against his ordination. I am not thinking of the sins which in some measure bind even the best among us, nor yet of faults which, hidden or grave, are yet not really incapacitating for the ministry. Of these we must all be conscious. "If we say that we have no sin, we deceive ourselves, and the truth is not in us. If we confess our sins, He is faithful and righteous to forgive us our sins, and to cleanse us from all unrighteousness." I have in my thought rather those degrading habits which, though secret and sometimes unsuspected, are really incapacitating, and would, if known, have been held to be prohibitive of ordination. The heaviest burden of the bishop's lot, and his greatest sorrow, arises from his unwitting ordination of men whom he subsequently discovers, when it is too late, were thus in themselves incapacitated for the Christian ministry. Great, indeed, are God's mercies, and who shall set bounds to His forgiveness? But there is a difference between a penitent sinner and a morally incapacitated minister: and here, on the threshold of ordination, we are considering fitness for the ministry.

It is essential that the aspirant to ordination should accept, honestly and with adequate knowledge, the doctrine and discipline of the Church from which he seeks the commission. This is the burden of most of the bishop's questions, of which the reasonableness and necessity are indisputable. Their honest answering, however, implies much thought and study. The substance of your answers is contained in the Declaration of Assent which you have already made, and in the Oath of Canonical Obedience which you will take immediately after your ordination. It would be insincere on my part if I affected to be ignorant of the difficulties which attach to these subscriptions, which may well perplex you, and which will provide you (if you are base enough to desire it) with pretexts for conduct which is not really congruous with loyalty. I am sure that in their broad intention the legal subscriptions are clear enough, and that, if in a spirit of dutifulness you seek to govern your practice by them, you will be little likely to go astray.

(3) *Competent knowledge.* To secure this is, of course, the main purpose of the examinations to

which you have been subjected. Here responsibility attaches to the Church, and to the bishop as the representative of the Church. We know, indeed, that examinations can at best be very rough and unsatisfactory tests of knowledge; but we have no other, and must needs therefore make use of them.

The vocation has been heard. You are sure that you heard it, and you have gone forward from step to step in a purpose that has ever gathered strength, until at last you have reached the final stage, and only wait for the commission which shall set the seal of God's acceptance on your self-surrender in obedience. And when the ordaining bishop to-morrow shall lay his hands on you, and in Christ's name give you authority to exercise your ministry in the Church of God, you will have full assurance that you are, indeed, "called and sent" to your sacred task. Think what all this means. Your work as Christ's ordained minister will be something vastly greater, stronger, more lasting than a personal venture of your own. Ordination binds that venture into the eternal purpose of the Almighty, and inspires it with the power of His Holy Spirit. Henceforward, as you humbly and honestly fulfil your duty, you are never alone. "I will not leave you comfortless: I will come to you." You enter into the tradition of apostolic witness, of redemptive ministry, of spiritual service, which has continued in gathering volume since that first ordination in the Upper Room, where Jesus, in the fresh glory of His Easter victory, Himself commissioned His servants – "As the Father sent Me even so send I you." You know yourselves to be very unworthy for so great an honour, very inadequate for so august a work, yet you dare not doubt that you shall be made both worthy and adequate. Like S. Peter, when he realised that he was verily in the presence of his true Lord, you would say, "Depart from me; for I am a sinful man, O Lord." And to you, as to S. Peter, in your penitence and dismay, shall be given the assurance, "Fear not; from henceforth thou shalt catch men."

VIII

*But Simon Peter, when he saw it, fell down at Jesus'
knees, saying, Depart from me; for I am a sinful man,
O Lord. . . . And Jesus said unto Simon, Fear not; from
henceforth thou shalt catch men.   And when they had
brought their boats to land, they left all, and followed Him.*

S. LUKE v. 8–11

YOU ARE ON THE THRESHOLD OF ORDINATION, and it
cannot but be the case that many challenging
thoughts are rising in your minds. Am I making a
mistake? Being what I know myself to be, and
having such a personal record as I know mine to be,
ought I to be ordained? Can I with a clear conscience answer that first and most searching of the
bishop's questions –

"Do you trust that you are inwardly moved by the
Holy Ghost to take upon you this office and ministration, to serve God for the promoting of His glory, and
the edifying of His people?"

The other questions are not so hard to answer.
Whatsoever difficulties attach to them have been
often raised, and as often answered. There is no lack
of casuistries which affect to reconcile men to their

pledges in ordination. Why should I be more scrupulous than my predecessors and contemporaries? But this first question goes deeper than the casuistries, and pushes its challenge in that innermost citadel of consciousness where God and His creature confront one another in naked and impenetrable solitude. Ought I verily to be ordained? What, when I cast aside all the covering veils of convention, is my motive in seeking ordination?

The analysis of motive is always difficult, often painful, sometimes baffling. We never really know ourselves. Only One knows us as we really are: "O Lord, Thou hast searched me out, and known me: Thou knowest my down-sitting, and mine up-rising; Thou understandest my thoughts long before. Thou art about my path, and about my bed: and spiest out all my ways. For lo, there is not a word in my tongue: but Thou, O Lord, knowest it altogether."

Motive is so oddly mingled, disguises itself so strangely, and varies so greatly in coercive power. It may be an overmastering conviction that thus and thus only may we rightly act; or, it may be the half-doubtful conclusion that, on the balance of considerations, such was the right course to follow. Motive may be largely dictated from without – the will of parents, the influence of a strong friendship, the earnest counsel of a superior, the pressure of circumstances, some personal liking for this or that

F

employment of the clergyman – and, throughout the whole process, one's own will may have been almost inactive, acquiescing in, rather than deliberately choosing, this way of life. Or, motive may be mainly from within – a clear call from God, ringing through the corridors of the spirit "like an increasing bell," always audible in the noise and strain of secular life, prevailing at last, and compelling obedience. What was my own motive? How did I come to be here looking forward to ordination in a few hours?

It is certain that many men are ordained who, as in later years becomes quite evident not only to others but also to themselves, had no adequate belief, no suitable character, no personal fitness for the clergyman's life. More and more it becomes apparent that the root of most pastoral failure – God alone knows how frequent and how pitiful it is – lies, not in the faults of our systems of discipline and patronage, though these are grave, but in the ordination of unsuitable men. The ordinal provides public challenges with respect to "any impediment or notable crime" in the candidates, but it is not often that the root of clerical incapacity lies in these. I have heard poor people say of their clergyman, not unkindly, for they sometimes add many kind words about him, "You see he's not a Christian"; and, in spite of the resentment which such a verdict cannot but arouse in a considering and charitable mind, we can see what is meant. These simple folk feel that their clergyman's central and continuing interest is not in his spiritual work. He can talk about sport, about politics, perhaps about art and literature, about plays and cinemas, even about finance, but about religion he is tongue-tied and embarrassed. There are, in fact, numerous clergymen in charge of parishes who have never realised religion as a personal experience, unique and masterful, the most real of all experiences, the most heart-searching, the most lastingly effective. The people are quick to recognise "a man of God."

The times are unfriendly to personal religion, very friendly to every form of externalism. It is a shallow age absorbed in trifling and transitory concerns, and even its deepest speculations are earth-born and earth-bound. The clergy also are the children of the age, and they perforce repeat its shibboleths and conform to its fashions. Their conceptions of spiritual duty shrink to the meagre limits of its demand. Professor Clement Webb has well described the age in its general character and broad effect:

"The true enemy of religion in the modern world is not philosophy or science; it is the purely secular habit of mind engendered in the hurrying life of great cities, where the heavens are veiled from view by the blaze of electric light and a display of many-coloured signs intended to advertise all manner of commercial enterprises is substituted for the solemn spectacle which Kant placed side by side with the moral law as an object of reverent awe; where the news of all the world is continually proclaimed by night and day and emphasised in proportion not to its true importance but to its journalistic effectiveness, and whence there is spread all over the globe, through the improvement of the means of communication, an external similarity of life among peoples of utterly different traditions, who are thus torn from their spiritual roots in the religious experience of their forefathers. To this secular habit it is probable that Christianity alone of the historical religions can hope to offer an effectual resistance."[1]

Such "effectual resistance" will never be offered by a secularised Christianity. The Church, which is ordained to be the "salt" and "light" of the world, will be apparently neither if "the salt has lost its savour," and the "light has been placed under a bushel." The clergy, in whom the Church's commission becomes explicit, illustrate conspicuously this condition of spiritual success. "Ye cannot serve God and mammon." If one conclusion more than any other "leaps to the eyes" of the student of ecclesiastical history, it is the moral and spiritual powerlessness of a secularised hierarchy. Yet it is precisely secularisation which in this secularist age is the most subtle and insistent danger to which the clergy are exposed.

More than ever, therefore, it is important that the clergy should themselves be genuinely Christians —

[1] v. *Religious Thought in England from 1850*, p. 185.

men in whose hearts is burning a passion for souls, who live habitually in touch with their Divine Redeemer, and in the midst of this difficult world, like Moses in Egypt, "endure as seeing Him who is invisible."

It is the eve of your ordination, and I would have you go to your great experience with a deep sense of personal unworthiness, and yet with an assured confidence and a quiet mind. There are certainly some considerations which may, and, in the case of every sincere man placed as you are now, ought to, counteract the self-distrust which apart from them might even be incapacitating.

First, then, remember that you are being called and sent to your work by a divinely appointed method, and in direct connection with a Divine purpose of mercy. You remember the conclusion to Bishop Lightfoot's great Dissertation on the Christian ministry. He has pointed out the sense in which the Christian minister may fairly be described and regarded as a priest, and thus he proceeds:

"According to this broader meaning, the priest may be defined as one who represents God to man and man to God. It is moreover indispensable that he should be called by God, for no man 'taketh this honour to himself.' The Christian ministry satisfies both these conditions.

"Of the fulfilment of the latter the only evidence within our cognisance is the fact that the minister is called according to a divinely appointed order. If the preceding investigation be substantially correct, the threefold ministry can be traced to Apostolic direction and short of an express statement we can possess no better assurance of a Divine appointment or at least a Divine sanction."

There is surely comfort in the thought that you have submitted yourself to the Church's judgment, satisfied the tests of fitness which the Church has laid down, and are to receive from the bishop's hands the commission which the Church is divinely authorised to give. For the Church is no merely human institution. It is, in the great description of S. Paul, Christ's body, "the fulness of Him that filleth all in all."

Next, you will remember that Almighty God reckoned (if I may so speak) with human weakness when He chose the method by which He would effect the world's redemption. Christ's Revelation of the Father was effected in and through the historic Incarnation. "For verily not of angels doth He take hold, but He taketh hold of the seed of Abraham. Wherefore it behoved Him in all things to be made like unto His brethren, that He might be a merciful and faithful High Priest in things pertaining to God, to make propitiation for the sins of the people. For in that He Himself hath suffered being tempted, He is able to succour them that are tempted." All through His earthly life the limitations of His self-chosen lot were urged by His contemporaries as inconsistent with His spiritual claim. "Is not this the Carpenter?" "Whence knoweth this Man letters, having never learned?" "By what authority doest Thou these things, and who gave Thee this authority?" "If Thou doest these things, manifest Thyself unto the world." His manner of living was too normal, too commonplace, too inconsistent with the conventional description of a religious leader. "The Son of Man came eating and drinking, and ye say, Behold a gluttonous man, and a winebibber, a friend of publicans and sinners." The clamour for "signs" which should authenticate His mission was persistent and increasing throughout His career. His refusal to satisfy it drew inevitably the final repudiation, "Not this man, but Barabbas!" "He was crucified through weakness," says S. Paul. This strange contradiction between the human limitations of the Incarnate and His Divine glory has been perpetuated *mutatis mutandis* in His Church. Christianity was to owe nothing to the power and persuasiveness of its human advocates. S. Paul's words to the Corinthians might be extended to the Church in every age, assuredly in our own: "For behold your calling, brethren, how that not many wise after the flesh, not many mighty, not many noble, are called: but God chose the foolish things of the world, that He might put to shame them that are wise: and God chose the weak things of the world, that He might put to shame the things that are strong: and the base things of the world, and the things that are despised, did God choose, Yea, and the things that are not, that He might bring to nought the things that are: that no flesh should glory before God." "We have the treasure in earthen vessels, that the exceeding greatness of the power may be of God, and not from ourselves."

And, lastly, never forget that Christ's religion is the religion of redemption. We believe – it is part of the Church's creed – "in the forgiveness of sins." Whatever may have been our faults and failures in the past – and much there must needs be which presses on us now with an insistence which chills, and confuses, and seems to disable – let us be very sure that "there is balm in Gilead." "If we say that we have no sin, we deceive ourselves and the truth is not in us: but if we confess our sins, He is faithful and righteous to forgive us our sins and to cleanse us from all unrighteousness." If we cast ourselves in lowly penitence at His feet, He will not reject us. "Lord, if Thou wilt, Thou canst make me clean," was the despairing cry of the "man full of leprosy," and the Saviour's answer to him is His answer still: "I will; be thou made clean."

Nor is it only, though this is much, that He accepts us, and binds up our broken hearts. There is a yet more wonderful potency in His absolution. He can

even transform our weakness into strength, give back
courage to the defeated, and restore to the penitent
the commission he seems to have for ever forfeited.
That moving record of S. Peter's fall and restoration
stands in the gospel as not only the perpetual rebuke
of self-confidence, but also as the perpetual prohibition of despair. "Godly sorrow worketh repentance,
a repentance which bringeth no regret, but the
sorrow of the world worketh death." The thrice-
repeated apostasy leads on, through the path of
penitence, to the thrice-repeated commission, for
love has returned to the wounded spirit and has
filled again the vacant shrine. "Peter was grieved
because He said unto him the third time, Lovest
thou Me? And he said unto Him, Lord, Thou
knowest all things; Thou knowest that I love Thee.
Jesus saith unto him, Feed My sheep." The sin,
renounced and forgiven, remains, no longer an
enfeebling memory, still less a beckoning finger
pointing ever the way to renewed transgression, but
a restraint on spiritual pride and a grace of understanding sympathy. "Before I was troubled," says
the psalmist, "I went wrong, but now have I kept
Thy word." That pathetic story of the Apostle who
was moved to an agony of self-disgust by the close
vision of the Saviour's power, and whose lamentable
prayer was answered by great words of mission, has
its counterpart still in the experience of many who
first realised their unworthiness on the threshold of

F*

their ordination, and then in ordination received restoration and assurance of faith: "But Simon Peter, when he saw it, fell down at Jesus' knees, saying, Depart from me: for I am a sinful man, O Lord. . . . And Jesus said unto Simon, Fear not; from henceforth thou shalt catch men."

IX

The end of the charge is love out of a pure heart and a good conscience and faith unfeigned: from which things some having swerved have turned aside unto vain talking.

i TIMOTHY i. 5, 6

IN A FEW HOURS you will have traversed one of the decisive experiences of your lives, the most decisive save only that which first brought home to you the reality and the significance of that discipleship to the Lord Jesus Christ to which in your baptism you were solemnly pledged. Ordination is much more than the entrance on a career, though it is that in a unique sense. But it is much more, because it sums up, formulates, and proclaims a spiritual purpose which has been present in the mind long before. Sometimes the notion of living one's life as a clergyman enters into the memories of childhood, becoming an assumption which has underlain the life of boyhood, and grown ever more definite as adolescence has passed into manhood. Sometimes the purpose was suggested at confirmation; and sometimes it has broken in on the mind suddenly at some moment of spiritual exaltation and self-discovery. To-morrow, you, who are to be ordained to the diaconate, will have to confess it publicly, when you make answer to the searching question which for you carries the whole spiritual validity of the following action:

"Do you trust that you are inwardly moved by the Holy Ghost to take upon you this Office and Ministration, to serve God for the promoting of his glory, and the edifying of his people?"

And you will make answer with the simple affirmative, "I trust so." You, who are to be ordained to the priesthood, will be answering once again the same question in your minds.

"Inwardly moved by the Holy Ghost" – the words must needs provoke thought. They indicate a process, and affirm its character. Something has been bearing on your mind which has created this resolution to be ordained, and that something was nothing merely natural, nothing external, but, within yourself, an influence from above, the moving of your will by the Holy Ghost. "The spirit of man is the candle of the Lord," wrote the Hebrew sage; and the Hebrew prophet, following out the implication of that sublime affirmation, did not scruple to clothe with Divine authority the promptings of the human conscience: "He hath showed thee, O man, what is good: and what doth the Lord require of thee, but to do justly, and to love mercy, and to walk humbly with thy God?"

For Christians the prophetic version of the nature

of man, and the prophetic doctrine of the conscience as the Vicar of God within him, are confirmed, interpreted, and developed by their belief in the Holy Spirit, as He has been revealed in the plenitude of His gracious power by Christ Himself. "The Spirit Himself beareth witness with our spirit, that we are children of God," writes S. Paul. The Christian life, from its start in the "new birth" to its final consummation in "glory," as the New Testament pictures it, is a supernatural thing, inspired, sustained, and carried to victory by the Spirit of God. "Walk by the spirit, and ye shall not fulfil the lust of the flesh," we are told, as if rightness of moral behaviour were the assured consequence of the Spirit's presence within the Christian. Again, "if ye are led by the Spirit, ye are not under the law," as if enfranchisement of soul were the sure result of obedience to the Spirit's rule. Once more, "As many as are led by the Spirit of God, these are sons of God," as if that inner submission to the Spirit carried the certain title to Divine sonship. You are not, therefore, to think ignobly of the movement of your mind which has led you to resolve to be ordained. The Christian, living of set purpose in the way of obedience, desiring sincerely to know God's will and to do it, and ever humbly praying for the guidance of the Holy Spirit, cannot be mistaken in clothing the resolution to seek Holy Orders, which finally establishes itself in his mind, with the character of a Divine direction, a calling by the Holy Ghost. The movement of the mind has ever gone along with the shaping of the life. Circumstance, Christianly regarded, is the obedient vassal of God's providence, and as it shapes itself harmoniously with the heart's desire, so that the purpose of ordination becomes – sometimes in the face of large difficulties – capable of accomplishment, the Christian finds exterior authentications of his interior persuasion, and owns himself without hesitation to be guided by the heavenly Father's love. Thus by degrees the consciousness of a vocation grows in the mind. "Fear not, little flock, it is your Father's good pleasure to give you the Kingdom," said Christ, and says still. It is not a vainglorious superstition, but the inevitable inference from our belief in God, as Jesus Christ has made Him known, that allows, nay compels, us to believe that our way in the world is not unmarked or unguided by Him; that for us, in our infinite littleness, there has been appointed a place in the scheme of His providence; and that He Himself, our Creator, has in His inscrutable wisdom called us to be His "fellow workers" in the achievement of His redemptive purpose for mankind. The authority of our Redeemer and the confirming experience of believers through so many ages unite to authenticate the words of the Sermon on the Mount, so wonderful and so consoling, which contradict flatly the hard wisdom of the world, and yet answer directly to the deepest requirements of our hearts in this tremendous hour: "Be not, therefore, anxious, saying, What shall we eat, or, What shall we drink? or, Wherewithal shall we be clothed? For after all these things do the Gentiles seek: for your heavenly Father knoweth that ye have need of all these things. But seek ye first His Kingdom, and His righteousness; and all these things shall be added unto you. Be not therefore anxious for the morrow: for the morrow will be anxious for itself. Sufficient unto the day is the evil thereof."

But may not motives be mixed? Assuredly, but that circumstance need not destroy the sincerity of the governing purpose, nor disallow our assurance of vocation. The desire to be ordained had necessarily to connect itself in your mind with the choice of a career or profession. It is God's ordinance for all of us that we should work, using faithfully the talents with which He has entrusted us, and rendering to Him in the end an account of our stewardship. Moreover, in the circumstances of the world, we must needs choose for ourselves the manner of our obedience to His will. What shall be our way of life? That is a question which we must all answer. A multitude of considerations will enter into the answer we return to it – personal preference, parental advice, physical health, mental capacity, temperamental suitability, congruity of circumstances. Some points must be settled for us; and some we must determine for ourselves. Our ultimate conviction that we have a vocation to the sacred ministry will be a resultant of many factors, the conclusion of a complicated and sometimes protracted process. "We have the treasure in earthen vessels, that the exceeding greatness of the power may be of God, and not from ourselves," says S. Paul, of the apostolic vocation; and the words hold of all spiritual ministry. The Divine call must be obeyed under the difficult conditions of life in the world, enabling us to earn our living honourably, and opening to us a professional career. What vistas of secularising worry, and de-spiritualising ambition are opened by the familiar phrases! The vocation, which we have dared to affirm, has been tested by the Church, so far as testing is now possible, since the gift of "discerning of spirits" has been long withdrawn, and the ordination proceeds. In due course the ordained man will be provided with a sphere within which he must exercise the ministry which he has received. In the ordination vows, which you will take to-morrow, when you make answer to the questions addressed to you before the laying-on of hands, the broad lines of your obligations are laid down. You will have pondered them long and anxiously; and I am well assured that your answers will be deliberate, intelligent, and resolutely sincere. May I, then, taking for granted both the genuineness of your vocation to the ministry, and the adequacy of your understanding

of the pledges which you will give, speak to you
shortly about some dangers which commonly beset
the clergyman, and which, in some form or other,
never cease to threaten his efficiency? The gist of
what I would desire to say has been said already,
with incomparable force and pathos, by S. Peter, in
a passage which might fairly be described as a
"charge" to all Christian ministers. Let me first
read it, and then make a few observations on its very
suggestive language: "The elders therefore among
you I exhort, who am a fellow-elder, and a witness
of the sufferings of Christ, who am also a partaker of
the glory that shall be revealed: tend the flock of
God which is among you, exercising the oversight,
not of constraint, but willingly, according unto God;
nor yet for filthy lucre, but of a ready mind: neither
as lording it over the charge allotted to you, but
making yourselves ensamples to the flock. And
when the Chief Shepherd shall be manifested, ye
shall receive the crown of glory that fadeth not away.
Likewise, ye younger, be subject unto the elder.
Yea, all of you gird yourselves with humility, to
serve one another: for God resisteth the proud, but
giveth grace to the humble. Humble yourselves
therefore under the mighty hand of God, that He
may exalt you in due time: casting all your anxiety
upon Him, because He careth for you. Be sober, be
watchful: your adversary the devil, as a roaring
lion, walketh about, seeking whom he may devour:

whom withstand stedfast in your faith, knowing that the same sufferings are accomplished in your brethren who are in the world. And the God of all grace, who called you unto His eternal glory in Christ, after that ye have suffered a little while, shall Himself perfect, stablish, strengthen you. To Him be the dominion for ever and ever. Amen."

The great Apostle, who here humbly places himself alongside of us as a "fellow-presbyter," indicates three types of moral failure as menacing the Christian minister: (i.) Lack of spontaneity in service; (ii.) Regarding the pastoral office from the hireling's point of view, as a way of gain; (iii.) Making spiritual office the occasion of personal claims. Let us look at these more carefully.

I. *All regular work tends to become mechanical*, to be performed as a matter of course with the unthinking facility bred of frequent repetition. This tendency, which makes for efficiency in the lower forms of human effort, is disastrous in the higher, and most disastrous of all in the highest. S. Peter's language is carefully designed to indicate the magnitude of the fault, and the secret of its correction. It is "the flock of God" that we are set to "tend," and our commission to pastorate is from Him. Two clauses, "exercising the oversight" and "according unto God," are textually doubtful, and are excluded from their text by Westcott and Hort, but they are strongly supported by the MSS., and have been retained by the revisers. We cannot be mistaken in recognising the Apostle's admonition to the presbyters as an echo of the admonition to himself, when three times over the risen Saviour had challenged him with the heart-piercing question, "Simon, son of John, lovest thou Me?" Then, in answer to his reiterated protestation, Christ had three times over renewed to him that pastoral commission which his treason might well have forfeited for ever: "Feed My lambs"; "Tend My sheep"; "Feed My sheep." The emphasis on the personal pronoun is noteworthy. It is love of the Master that must provide the motive of pastorate. It is the Master's ownership of the "flock" that shall make it dear to the pastor's heart. And this is the suggestion of the clause, "according unto God." "Tend the flock of God that is among you not of constraint but willingly like God." Let your pastorate be on the Divine model, a pastorate of self-surrendering love. Two circumstances of your work will make lack of spontaneity in your service perilously easy. On the one hand, you will commonly work by yourself. On the other hand, you will often work in an atmosphere which is by no means favourable to the maintenance of a high standard of pastoral effort. The considerable reduction in the number of unbeneficed clergymen has made the existence of staffs of clergy, even in large parishes, very occasional. Most commonly the deacon has no fellow curates to keep him up to the mark by a generous emulation. Often he is set to work in a separate district where he is very much his own master, and has but slight contact even with the incumbent under whom he works. There is little expectation in the people that he shall be regular and devout, little desire that he shall be zealous in spiritual effort, a ready condonation of slackness and secularity. What Bishop Walsham How once said was a heavy disadvantage to choristers – that they had a deadening familiarity with spiritual things – is also, and in larger measure, true of clergymen. When once spontaneity has gone out of his work, and he goes through his course of sacred duty as a matter of necessary routine, putting no spiritual intention into the hallowed language, and feeling no inward response to the prescribed devotions, the clergyman is in grave peril of accepting as natural and inevitable the low standard of ministry to which he has fallen. Be very watchful, therefore, against acquiescing in your own failure. Much is gained if you can perceive and lament your fault. You will prevail against it if you keep your private religion a living thing, vitalised by contact, ever renewed in prayer and sacrament, with the Chief Shepherd, whose representative you are, and whose example is the model of your pastorate. And as a protection against a perfunctory habit, I think that personal intercourse with a spiritually minded friend is of great value. You will be unfortunate indeed if you can find none

in the neighbourhood where you work, no fellow
clergyman to whom you may bring the help which
you seek from him, no spiritually minded layman,
who can commune with you about the things of
Christ. You will be unwise if you do not make full
use of such friendship as you find.

II. *The Hireling's point of view.* μηδὲ αἰσχροκερδῶς;
the adverb is here only used in the New Testament.
In the Epistle to Titus we read that one mark of
the "unruly men" who were troubling the Cretan
Church was "teaching things that they ought not for
filthy lucre's sake." It is full of sinister suggestiveness
that every English incumbent on his institution to
a benefice, is required to make a declaration against
simony. His appointment, if it is to be legally valid,
must have been free from taint of bribery. I need
not remind you how dark a shadow on the Church's
life from the first this lust of "filthy lucre" among the
clergy has been. It is already prominent in the New
Testament; it gathers importance as the Church
emerges out of the ages of persecution into the
perilous popularity of Establishment; from time to
time it breaks out in prodigious scandals; it remains
one of the besetting sins of the modern Church. The
language of S. Peter, says Dr. Bigg, "implies that the
presbyter was in receipt of a stipend, otherwise it
would have been impossible for him to take a hireling's view." "Peter," comments Dr. Moffatt, "pro-
tests against mercenary aims, against the temper

which makes men do no more than they are paid for." Will anyone who knows the actual working of the parochial system doubt the prevalence of that temper among the clergy? Two circumstances of our time do certainly encourage it. The triumph of what is called "democracy" is carrying the "trade-union" point of view into general acceptance. Many of the clergy are drawn from those sections of society in which trade unionism is the dominant social factor, and they find it very easy to think of their ministry in terms of the trade-union ethic. Moreover, the poverty of the clergy has had the effect of emphasising quite disastrously the financial aspects of their professional life. "Ye cannot serve God and mammon," said our Master, and, when the impossible dualism is attempted by the Christian minister, the effect must needs be spiritually ruinous. I incline to place considerations, which may rightly be summed up in the sinister phrase "filthy lucre," very high among the disabling faults of the modern English clergy. The poverty of the clergy is a very grave fact, but we may not allow it to ensnare us in this vice of "covetousness" which, as S. Paul tells us, is "idolatry." Two counsels would seem suitable even to the case of the poorest clergyman : first, keep out of debt; next, think as little about money as possible. The clergyman's independence is essential to the quality and reputation of his ministry. A man who doesn't pay his debts can never be independent, and will hardly long remain honest. He certainly will not be respected. Remember, this prosaic matter of "making both ends meet" with a small income is precisely the practical problem which most of your parishioners will be facing for themselves, often in circumstances even harder than yours. They will inevitably judge you by your success in solving it. The clergyman in debt is always thinking about money, watching for opportunities to make money, apt to sink into a mendicant habit which is corrosive of self-respect. Therefore, bind it upon your conscience as a primary obligation of your ministry to keep out of debt. I dare say you wonder why I should think it necessary to bring into my charge such a commonplace subject as keeping out of debt. You would not wonder if you knew as much as a bishop has to know about the indebtedness of the clergy, and the sad spiritual failures which flow from it. We are not as clergymen entitled to make money out of our ministry. A sufficient maintenance is all that we may rightly claim, and a sufficient maintenance in the Church of England, as a general rule, we shall receive. We were not appointed to our spiritual work on trade-union principles. We do not work under trade-union rules. We have no limited hours and guaranteed minima of remuneration; but we have publicly declared our resolve to "follow Christ in the way," and all our time and all our powers are His.

III. *Basing personal pretensions on spiritual office.*
"Neither as lording it over the charge allotted to
you." Many a clergyman who is far removed from
the vulgar temptations of "filthy lucre" is easily
ensnared by personal ambition, which is none the less
sinful for being disguised in lofty terms of official
claim. It is a real danger to the newly ordained man.
As a clergyman you become in the district where you
live a public personage; in the congregation where
you minister you must needs be a leading figure.
Take care not to presume on that position, which is
solely connected with your office, and implies no
kind of merit in yourself. The affectation of superiority is peculiarly offensive when observed in
clergymen who are young, inexperienced, and
nowise distinguished either by gifts or attainments.
Some observations of Dr. Moffatt are worth our
thinking over. He quotes a layman's protest against
clerical assumption. Nowadays a mature layman
will resent a clergyman calling

"me one of his sheep. I am not a sheep relatively to
him. I am at least his equal in knowledge, and greatly
his superior in experience. Nobody but a parson would
venture to compare me to an animal (such a stupid
animal too!) and himself to that animal's master."

There is something in the layman's repugnance.
That monopoly of education and even of power
which once belonged to the clergy gave a meaning

to the high-sounding titles by which Christ's ministers are conventionally described, which they no longer carry. In other words, we have to win men's respect by our service; we cannot any more claim it for our recognised superiority. Humility rooted in penitence and sustained by discipline will secure you against this particular fault of arrogance. But enough. God Himself, who has called you to this ministry, will make you able to fulfil it. "He is faithful that promised." Do not doubt that you are His concern, and that He means your final victory. Commit yourselves in penitent faith into His hands, and go forward with a good courage. "Humble yourselves therefore under the mighty hand of God, that He may exalt you in due time: casting all your anxiety upon Him; because He careth for you."

X

Who can tell how oft He offendeth? O cleanse Thou me from my secret faults. Keep Thy servant also from presumptuous sins, lest they get the dominion over me: so shall I be undefiled, and innocent from the great offence. Let the words of my mouth, and the meditation of my heart, be alway acceptable in Thy sight, O Lord, my strength, and my redeemer.

PSALM xix. 12–15

YOU HAVE REACHED the end of your preparation for Holy Orders, and have now come to the threshold of that decisive experience. It is a solemn moment for you and for me. Of all the duties of a bishop none is more critically important, and none is more intrinsically difficult, than that which belongs to him as a man charged with "publick authority given unto him in the Congregation to call and send Ministers into the Lord's Vineyard." For if he err in the fulfilment of that duty, his error is irreparable, and must be widely mischievous. Of all the disabling shadows which rest on the Church's life, none is so dark as that which is cast by unworthy ministers. And, perhaps, no greater misfortune can befall any young man than to commit himself to the career of a Christian minister, if he be not indeed "inwardly moved by the Holy Ghost" to seek ordination. A

186

cruel wrong is inflicted on the man who is admitted to Holy Orders without careful weighing of character and qualifications. That is the bishop's burden. He can but humbly and honestly face his obligation, taking every precaution within his reach, and ever depending on that assistance of the Spirit of God, which Christ has promised to His servants when they invoke it in the way of His service.

To-night, then, I want to speak to you some words of counsel and warning, which you will not easily forget. As the bishop from whom you will receive the great commission, I can claim your respectful attention. As one who to-morrow will complete forty-four years of ministry,[1] I must needs speak with the authority of long experience: as addressing you on the eve of your ordination, I can count upon your close and anxious audience. I have set down seven counsels, which may well appear to you obvious and commonplace, but which appear to me to be relevant, requisite, and really important.

I. *Be watchful against the known, and even notorious, faults of the time.* Let me instance but three – reckless talking, belittlement of religious observances, and contempt for authority.

(*a*) Older men like myself are amazed at the licence of speech which now prevails. There is a profaneness and indecency now common in social intercourse which certainly would not have been

---

[1] This charge was delivered in 1931.

tolerated in our youth. I do not think that men were more hypocritical then than they are now, nor do I think it wholly reasonable to suppose that men now are more irreligious and unclean than they were then; but I must needs think that the standard of conversation has deteriorated woefully, and I cannot but fear that the change will tell badly on character. Read Bishop Butler's sermon "On the Government of the Tongue," and you will not be disposed to underrate the gravity of reckless and lewd talking. Remember the words of Christ which we who bear His commission cannot afford to forget. He connects the quality of a man's speech with the state of his heart so closely that He declares that the final judgment will turn on the evidence provided by conversation: "How can ye, being evil, speak good things? For out of the abundance of the heart the mouth speaketh. The good man out of his good treasure bringeth forth good things: and the evil man out of his evil treasure bringeth forth evil things. And I say unto you, that every idle word that men shall speak, they shall give account thereof in the day of judgment. For by thy words thou shalt be justified, and by thy words thou shalt be condemned."

(b) Do not yourselves indulge in the modern fashion of belittling religious observances, nor give the impression that you concur with it. There are few compliments which the clergyman should distrust more on the lips of worldly men than that which describes him as "broad-minded." When all is said, there are worse things than what society gibes at as "sabbatarianism," and "superstition," and "narrow-mindedness." Unless the Gospels carry no message to the modern Church, we are as disciples, and *a fortiori* as ministers of Christ, pledged to such a public profession of our religious allegiance as will not wholly accord with the standards, values, and habits of Vanity Fair. Nor can it be seriously contended, though it is often assumed, that a total abstinence from religious observances, such as is now becoming fashionable, is the most convincing evidence of intelligent faith, or genuine piety, or religious tolerance, or loyal discipleship. It is our duty to commend our spiritual message by every legitimate means, but we may not carry our propitiating procedures to the length of disguising it altogether, like that "soft dean" in the XVIIIth century who, preaching at Court, shrank from a direct reference to the final fate of impenitent sinners, but threatened the sinner with punishment in "a place which he thought it not decent to name in so polite an assembly."

(*c*) The modern habit of "speaking evil of dignitaries," belittling the commands of superiors, and affecting an independence which is exempt from discipline, sits ill on a clergyman, who is in society as the apostle and embodied symbol of authority. "Sin is lawlessness," says S. John, and S. Paul states the same truth from another point of view, when he reminds the Corinthians that "God is not a God of confusion, but of peace." It is difficult to over-estimate the loss of moral influence which has be-fallen the English clergy from no other cause than their own lack of discipline and contempt of lawful authority.

II. *Be careful to take a just measure of yourself.* It has been observed that the English clergyman is often marked by an autocratic and even domineer-ing manner, which could never be seemly in the servant of Christ, and sometimes accords ill with his actual claims to deference and submission. I think the explanation lies not so much in the clergyman's fault as in the unwholesome conditions of his official life. In his parish the incumbent has no immediate superior. In an industrial parish he will have the grave disadvantage of living mostly among his intellectual inferiors. To an extent which is exceptional, and by no means wholesome, he will find himself associated with women. When he visits the people, he will find the wife at home far more often than the husband. His district visitors and Sunday-school teachers will mostly be women. The bulk of his congregation and the majority of his communicants will be women. His annual sale of work will be mostly carried through by women. It is mere matter of fact that the parish clergyman lives in female society far more than is good for him. The

social atmosphere thus created is favourable to
clerical self-assertion, for women are apt to invite
and accept masculine dominance. To deprecate
this abnormal association with women in clerical
life is certainly to say nothing derogatory to women
as such. It would be not less unwholesome, though
in a different way, if the clergyman were shut up
mainly to the society of men. My point is that the
clergyman's official duty commonly involves him in
an unwholesomely exaggerated association with one
sex. Add to all this the extraordinary freedom from
oversight that the clergyman enjoys, the perilous
security of his tenure of office, the absence from his
normal experience of any effective criticism, and
you can see how easily he may acquire an exaggerated estimate of his own importance, and indulge
a domineering temper. Cultivate, therefore, the
habit of self-criticism. Look at your own defects;
consider your own failures; repent of your own sins.
"Be not wise in your own conceits," writes S. Paul;
and S. Peter is very insistent: "Yea, all of you gird
yourselves with humility, to serve one another: for
God resisteth the proud, but giveth grace to the
humble. Humble yourselves therefore under the
mighty hand of God, that He may exalt you in due
time: casting all your anxiety upon Him, because
He careth for you."

III. *Be loyal to the Church of England.* It is only as
a member of the Church of England that you have

become a member of the Holy Catholic Church. It is only by being loyal to the Church of England that you can be loyal to the Catholic Church. To distinguish between the two, as if there were a choice before you, is all one with setting your notion of what membership of the Catholic Church requires above that which the Church of England affirms. Loyalty means something more than a reluctant abstinence from specific breaches of the Church's rules. It cannot mean less than a deliberate acceptance, a harmony of spirit, a careful concern for the Church's interest and honour. You will not merely promise to obey your lawful superiors, but to obey them "reverently," not merely to "follow their godly admonitions," but to do so "with a glad mind and will." Such obedience implies much more than a mechanical and reluctant submission. It assumes such a frank acceptance of the authority of the Church of England as will clothe its requirements with a clear title to your loyal regard. Loyalty can hardly consist with a deliberate departure from the Church's language and custom. When, for example, a clergyman allows himself to speak of the Holy Communion as "the Mass," he not only startles and alienates many of his people, but he breaks away from the accustomed usage of the Church of England, and dishonours it before the world. He lets the parish know that he sets his own preference before the settled practice of the Church, and invites the people

to follow him rather than the Church. Again, it is
not really consistent with loyalty to the Church of
England so to order the ecclesiastical life of the parish
that the people fall out of line with their fellow
churchmen, and perforce become an isolated unit
within the diocese. This congregationalism (for it is
nothing else) cannot be redeemed by being styled
"Catholic," for it sins against the very spirit of
Catholicism, and stamps parochial life with a
sectarian character. The ill usage of the *Church
Times* is being copied in the parishes, and colours the
language of choir-boys and servers.

In a recent issue that newspaper informed its
readers that "of the forty-three English diocesans"
"not more than ten can be possibly regarded as
Catholic." Charles Simeon once gave a precise
number of the Christians whom he could find in
Cambridge. The arrogant uncharity of such language is only matched by its intrinsic absurdity:
but I am concerned now with the spirit which it
expresses, and which has other and not less deplorable expressions.

IV. *Keep in charity with your colleagues.* It is the
lamentable fact that the work of Christ in the
parishes is often grievously hampered by the
strained relations of the clergy with one another.
Remember that continuing resentments are spiritually paralysing. The people are quick to discern
their presence, and to discount the clergyman's

G

influence by his known disposition. Here let me press on you two necessary rules. First, never talk about your differences or grievances with parishioners. Inevitably you will choose for your confidences those whose agreement you can count upon. Therefore, you will confirm yourself in your own position, which may be ill chosen and really indefensible. Moreover you will certainly create a focus of scandal, from which great evils may come. Next, avoid the foolish but frequent practice of writing to your vicar, instead of going to see him, when any misunderstanding or disagreement arises. Letter-writing is a form of cowardice. Many a man is valorous with a pen who daren't face the man he writes to. In what I am now saying, you will recognise that I am speaking of what I know to be actually happening in the diocese. To write, and set out your case, is to organise yourself for conflict: *lex scripta manet*. If your vicar be foolish enough to write in reply, a correspondence begins which inevitably deteriorates in tone and temper. Moreover, your vanity will certainly lead you to show your own compositions to others; and so the area of the strife will be ever growing wider. And all the while both men's minds are shadowed and distracted by uncharitable thoughts; and they carry to their work and to their worship that which goes far to ruin both. Almost always these differences between the clergy would be cleared away by frank discussion; and if such frank discussion be not possible between them, then I leave you to judge what measure of fraternity is present in their hearts. It needs not that I should speak of the personal unhappiness which darkens life when the shadow of discord falls between colleagues. "If, therefore, thou art offering thy gift at the altar, and there rememberest that thy brother hath aught against thee, leave there thy gift before the altar, and go thy way, first be reconciled to thy brother and then come and offer thy gift." God's blessing can never rest on quarrelling clergy, and on its invariable concomitant, a divided parish.

V. *Don't underrate the importance of your own example.* The clergyman is a very conspicuous figure on the parochial stage. He is always in view, for whether at work in the parish, visiting the parishioners in their houses, teaching in the schools, taking the lead in parochial functions, or officiating in the parish church and churchyard, he stands out to the general view. His official character implies a personal discipleship. He is assumed to be a Christian because he is known to be a Christian minister. Accordingly, his behaviour is expected to be congruous with this assumption. In some sense he becomes the authorised commentary on the message he delivers. Fuller's quaint language carries a sound doctrine well worthy of our attention:

"In some persons gravity is most necessary. – Namely, in magistrates and ministers. One Palavizine, an Italian gentleman, and kinsman to Scaliger, had in one night all his hair changed from black to grey. Such an alteration ought there to be in the heads of every one that enters into holy orders or public office, – metamorphosed from all lightness to gravity."[1]

I have already referred to the loose language now so common among us. This habit is very catching, and, unless the clergyman be careful, he may drift into it almost unwittingly. But let him make no mistake. Words that are taken as a matter of course from the lips of a layman are felt to be unworthy and even shocking on the lips of a clergyman. Dr. Johnson found the merriment of parsons to be "mighty offensive." I assume that his reverent and deeply religious mind was offended by such noisy and unrestrained jocosity as disclosed a reckless and undisciplined habit. Many clergymen are free-masons, and as such attend the lodge dinners. They should be particularly careful how they bear themselves on these occasions. Let them not forget that they are responsible, not only for their conduct, but for the impression which their conduct makes.

"Take thought for things honourable in the sight of all men," says S. Paul. The clergyman makes a bad bargain when he buys a reputation for good fellowship at the price of creating a suspicion of inebriety. The suspicion may be groundless, but it will cast a weakening spell on all his work none the

[1] v. *The Holy State* : " Of Gravity."

less. Be sure that your private habits – the time when you get up and when you go to bed, the books you read, and the company you keep, the regularity with which you pay your bills, and the quality of your family life – will all be well known, and rigorously weighed in the parish. No public performances can make up for private failures. Your preaching will be read in the light of your practice, and men will not long endure a contradiction between the two. We are "soldiers on service" in an enemy's country, and it is not safe for us to relax vigilance and grow careless of discipline. "Wherefore let him that thinketh he standeth take heed lest he fall. There hath no temptation taken you but such as man can bear: but God is faithful, who will not suffer you to be tempted above that ye are able; but will with the temptation make also the way of escape, that ye may be able to endure it."

VI. *Throw yourself frankly into the life of the diocese.* Every fault is stimulated by isolation, and many auxiliaries to duty are lost. The spirit of service is the spirit of fraternity, and that spirit grows strong in fellowship with the brethren. You may not rightly limit your obligations to the parish where you are appointed to serve. The rural dean will summon you to the chapters of the deanery. You are bound to obey that summons. The bishop will convene you for purposes of general reference, you are bound to appear before him. Don't give to party what is due to the Church. The less you have to do with partisan organisations the better; but the more frankly you give yourself to the life of the Church the happier and more serviceable will your ministry become. Self-woven isolation is the source of much clerical failure.

VII. *Don't think about preferment and remuneration.* Nothing so degrades the Christian ministry as the prominence given to matters which the Apostles were wont roughly to indicate by the ugly phrase "filthy lucre." Nothing so commends the clergyman's ministry as the fact that he is seen to be, in the true sense of the word, unworldly. There is no more weakening disposition than discontent, and yet how common it is! Surely it is as irrational as it is enfeebling. In the Church of England the clergy have assigned to them official incomes, small for the most part, but hardly ever so small as to be really insufficient. Anyway, we did not fix them, but we knew what they would be when we accepted them. We must live within them, and be content to do so. Let us remember that it is no mean privilege to have an income which, albeit small, is secure. It sets us free from the daily worries which afflict so great a proportion of our fellow citizens. Let us take full advantage of our privilege, and give ourselves whole-heartedly to our spiritual work. If we believe in God's providence, we know that He will direct our course. Only let us "seek first His Kingdom and His righteousness" and we may leave the future in

His hands. Let me repeat the seven counsels which I have thought fit to offer you, and which I charge you to heed:

I. Be watchful against the known, and even notorious, faults of the time.

II. Be careful to take a just measure of yourself.

III. Be loyal to the Church of England.

IV. Keep in charity with your colleagues.

V. Don't underrate the importance of your own example.

VI. Throw yourself frankly into the life of the diocese.

VII. Don't think about preferment and remuneration.

There is much more that I should like to say to you, but there is no time. I have said enough to warn you of some pitfalls which you must be careful to avoid. Let me end my charge by reminding you that, however grave the risks and difficulties of our ministry may be (and that they are very great I cannot doubt), we have access to spiritual resources which are more than adequate to all our needs. "Lo, I am with you alway, even unto the end of the world." That promise is ever made good to Christ's servants. The secret of spiritual victory lies in a discipleship which is sincere, humble, and obedient. We, too, may learn the truth which S. Paul learned in the same school of sorrowful experience as is ours –

the truth that "His power is made perfect in weakness." It is when our official ministry parts company with our personal allegiance that we are in danger of every kind of failure. So long as the two are held together, we cannot really fail, because our public witness is seen and felt to spring from a personal conviction which must utter itself thus. "Hereby shall we know that we are of the truth, and shall assure our hearts before Him, whereinsoever our heart condemn us: because God is greater than our heart, and knoweth all things. Beloved, if our heart condemn us not, we have boldness towards God: and whatsoever we ask, we receive of Him, because we keep His commandments, and do the things that are pleasing in His sight."

May God be with you at this time of solemn self-surrender! purging your purpose from every taint of self-seeking, strengthening your wills for the task before you, filling your hearts with the sure sense of vocation, heard and obeyed, and giving you in rich measure the strength and comfort of His Holy Spirit!

"Almighty Father, we thank Thee for that Thou hast given us the will to serve Thee in the Ministry of Thy Holy Church, and we pray Thee to complete in us the good work which Thou hast begun. Purify our motives: strengthen our purpose: quicken our zeal: kindle our affections. Take away from our hearts whatsoever is contrary to Thy Will, and give us peace in Thy service, through Jesus Christ our Lord. Amen."

XI

Set not your mind on high things,
but condescend to things that are lowly.

ROMANS xii. 16

And whatsoever ye do, in word or in deed, do all in the
name of the Lord Jesus, giving thanks to God the Father
through Him.

COLOSSIANS iii. 17

THE WORD συναπαγόμενοι rendered "condescend"
is in the margin of the Revised Bible rendered "be
carried away with," and that perhaps best conveys
S. Paul's meaning. He bids us be verily enthusiastic
over our evident and immediate duties, which, just
because they are evident and immediate, are likely to
be little esteemed and readily neglected. There is no
contradiction here with another Pauline admonition
– "Seek those things that are above : set your minds
on things above, where Christ is." This admonition
has reference to the settled habit of the Christian's
mind. It is equivalent to the Apostle's exhortation
to the Thessalonians to "pray without ceasing." He
could not mean a perpetual exercise of formal prayer,
but points to that conscious dependence on God, and
realisation of His presence, at all times and in all
places, which is the rightful temper of disciples.

In every kind of human labour two conditions of efficiency are generally recognised. There must be attention to detail, or, which comes to the same thing, concentration on immediate tasks; and the workman must rejoice in his work, for only so will he put into it his best intelligence and his most conscientious effort. We may say with truth that the higher and more difficult the work may be, the more plainly do these conditions of efficiency hold good.

Let us apply these general observations to the specific matter of the Christian ministry, which you are shortly to receive as your life's concern. I will set out what I desire to say to you in three propositions:

I. *God's claim to our service is expressed primarily in the demands of daily duty.* Until these are satisfied, we cannot serve Him acceptably in our sacred office. You will recall the terrible words of the Sermon on the Mount in which Christ pictures Himself rejecting as "workers of iniquity" professed disciples who had been conspicuously successful in religious work. "Many will say to Me in that day, Lord, Lord, did we not prophesy by Thy name, and by Thy name cast out devils and by Thy name do many mighty works? And then will I profess unto them, I never knew you: depart from Me ye that work iniquity." Religious work may easily grow to be a snare to us; and if, as is generally our case, it carry us into situations of prominence and publicity, and draw upon us much observation and, it may be, even much general applause and admiration, it may readily cheat us into failing to perceive, or even condoning, grave and even gross paradoxes of conduct. The philanthropist John Howard, whose praise is in all the churches, and who was certainly a man of high character and noble disinterestedness, was yet cruelly indifferent to his duty towards his unfortunate child. In the repulsive character of Pecksniff, a man who was always uttering sentiments of exalted morality, and who none the less was, in his personal habit, a greedy and heartless man, Dickens has drawn a familiar picture. The clergy, who are professionally required to be frequently using the language of devotion, and are set to press on others the obligations of religion, are peculiarly exposed to the temptation of tolerating that dissidence between profession and practice which is the essence of hypocrisy. In his powerful but intensely repulsive novel, *Elmer Gantry*, the well-known American writer, Sinclair Lewis, has drawn the portrait of the professional evangelist who treats "godliness" as "a way of gain," and prostitutes his abilities to his own material advantage. He has drawn a caricature, but a successful one – that is, a caricature which has an indisputable resemblance to fact. The great importance of the clergyman's home is directly connected with the character of the home as the scene of men's most natural self-expression. The story was current of my famous predecessor, Bishop Cosin, that his only son said with respect to him, that "he would rather trail a pike in a regiment of foot soldiers than live at home with his father." It would appear, if that story does not malign the bishop, that his life at home was in apparent discord with his public character. With regard to the normal continuing obligations of life, the Apostle's words have relevance: "Set not your mind on high things, but condescend to things that are lowly."

II. *The faithful performance of immediate duties is the remedy of lop-sidedness in religion,* for lop-sidedness has its principal root in the indulgence of personal preferences. Lop-sidedness is a dark shadow on clerical life. There are many types of lop-sided clergymen. Five are sufficiently familiar. (1) The Academic. This was once numerous in the days of clerical fellowships. It flourished in college livings, and was favoured by the difficulty of communications which severed remote rural parishes from the main course of public life. This type is vanishing from the world. (2) The Political. Parsons who make the pulpit the instrument for publishing their political opinions are now numerous, and for reasons which are sufficiently obvious. By preaching politics they can count on pleasing all who share their opinions. But, unhappily, clergymen, being as a rule inexperienced in political affairs and professionally accustomed to be dogmatic, are always likely to carry into their politics a passion and a lack of proportion beyond what is common among laymen.

Thus, not only are political opponents offended by what they regard, not without reason, as unfair behaviour, but the general public is offended by extravagant language. (3) The Fanatic. This type of lop-sided clergyman is generally found in the advocates of some cause which has come to be the alpha and omega of his preaching, e.g. teetotalism, sexual purity, foreign missions, adventism, modernism, groupism, and the like. The cause may be excellent in itself, but, kept always in the centre, it blocks out other, and perhaps better, things, and distorts the perspectives of ministry. (4) The Religious Partisan. Generally a member of a party organisation, E.C.U., or C.A., or M.C.U., and a close student of the party journal. I could wish that the clergy would treat all ecclesiastical newspapers as the Ephesians, in an access of repentance, treated their curious books. Just now this type of lop-sided clergyman is much in evidence. (5) The Social Reformer. A man who often reimburses himself for the decay of his interest in things of the Spirit by his concentration on mundane business. Often a useful citizen, but always a bad parson, more familiar with the Housing Acts than with the Bible, and more at home in a municipal council chamber than in the House of God.

III. *"Set not your mind on high things, but condescend to things that are lowly."* *Neglect of S. Paul's counsel is the explanation of the singular paradox with which we of the*

Church of England are but too familiar – a fervid advocacy of Catholicism combined in the same clergyman with an obstinate disobedience to authority. "Mind not high things" – that is, don't trouble yourself about large questions of ecclesiastical theory and organisation; "but condescend to things that are lowly" – that is, give yourself whole-heartedly· to the duties which belong to your position. S. Paul probably had in his view theological speculations such as those connected with justification, election, and predestination, which are the substance of most of the Epistle to the Romans, and views about the Second Advent of the Redeemer, which had a great fascination for the believers of the first ages. These questions, difficult, abstract, and remote from life, led but too easily to idleness as in Thessalonica, or to disputation as in Galatia, or to scandal as in Corinth. Students of English literature will recall the passage in *Paradise Lost*, in which Milton, a keen controversialist in a controversial age, pictured the fallen angels in hell as engaged in theological speculations:

> "Others apart sat on a hill retired,
> . In thoughts more elevate, and reason'd high
> Of providence, foreknowledge, will and fate,
> Fix'd fate, free will, foreknowledge absolute:
> And found no end, in wandering mazes lost.
> Of good and evil much they argued then,
> Of happiness and final misery,
> Passion and apathy, and glory and shame:
> Vain wisdom all, and false philosophy."

"Dolus latet in generalibus" – "self-deception is disguised by the zeal for large disputations." You remember how the Samaritan harlot endeavoured to turn aside the question of her own evil living by raising the hotly debated issue of the right place "where God ought to be worshipped." Christian history contains many examples of keen theologians who were ill-living men; and assuredly a most punctilious concern for the ceremonial of religious worship may consist with a low standard of personal morality. The old pagan severance of religion from morality has its roots deep in our nature, and is ever seeking to assert itself. Alexander VI was the most infamous of the popes of the Renaissance, yet his contemporaries noted with admiration the unusual concern which he displayed for the regular and splendid performance of the public offices of religion.

The "lowly things" of the Christian ministry – house-to-house visitation, teaching in Bible classes and Sunday-schools, bringing the people to public worship, relieving the poor, ministering to the sick – are often unattractive and even repulsive. Their performance seems to attract little attention, and is recompensed by little praise. Yet in the faithful carrying out of these tasks lies the essence of genuine pastorate. The clergyman must seek grace from God to make him able to overcome his shyness, or indolence, or ambition, and to see these "lowly things" of his duty transfigured into Divine service.

"Whatsoever ye do, do all in the name of the Lord Jesus, giving thanks to God the Father through Him."

In one of his novels Dickens introduces the character, half-comic, half-serious, of a man whose buoyant spirits found a stimulus to effort and cheerfulness in the most difficult and distressing circumstances. Mark Tapley's attitude is worth considering. What the natural optimism of an exuberant nature did for him, that his religious interpretation of his duty ought to do for the parson. Like Moses he must "endure as seeing Him who is invisible." Set it before yourselves, as the object of your ambition, to become efficient. The career before you is that of the parish clergyman. These first years of ministry are your apprenticeship, and you will have spent them ill if you haven't succeeded in mastering the business to which you are to devote your life. By "mastering your business" I do not of course mean that you will have nothing more to learn. I suppose the longest experience of pastoral ministry, and the highest efficiency in the work, will leave the Christian minister with the consciousness that he is but beginning to understand what Christian pastorate means. But I do mean that, in these first years of his apprenticeship, the young clergyman ought to learn what are the right lines of effort, what are the best proved methods of work, and what are the pitfalls against which he must be watchful. He ought during these first years of apprenticeship to discover something definite and trustworthy about his own capabilities. You will all have special aptitudes which you must seek to develop; but an efficient clergyman must be what is colloquially called an "all-round man." There will be work which you will do best in youth (perhaps can only do then), and other work which you will do better as you garner experience; but you cannot rightly or wisely shut out any part of the parson's work from your concern. If you are so fortunate as to be licensed to a parish where the incumbent is a wise, devout, and sympathetic man, be sure and make as much use as you can of the opportunity of learning which you will have received. Avoid the tacit assumption of omniscience which too often marks the newly ordained clergyman. Your task is to become efficient, and your business now is to learn, as presently it will be your duty to teach. Books can teach something, but men can teach more. Be ready to learn. If joy in work is one great condition of efficient working, discontent is as certainly a great condition of failure. Discontent is terribly common among the clergy. Discontent with ourselves may be a very wholesome thing; but discontent with our circumstances is always a very disabling thing; and discontent with our duty must always be a very sinful thing. Give as little thought to money as possible. The worst-paid clergyman has more than he deserves, and far more than men far greater and holier than he have had. Give no thought to what is called preferment. If you are efficient, you will have all the preferment you can reasonably expect. Give yourself without reserve to your ministry, and put your trust in God.

Nearly fifty years[1] have passed since I was myself ordained in Cuddesdon Parish Church on a lovely summer morning in June 1887. How well I remember the tumult of conflicting thoughts which raged in my mind, and perhaps hindered me from entering as fully as I would have entered into the solemn yet exalting service! How little I guessed what lay before me! The immense failures which would overtake my too-ardent beginnings; the disappointments which would shadow my later course; the growing sense of inadequacy which would become a settled resident in my mind. The happiest years of my ministry were those in which, as the vicar of a great industrial parish, I was nearest to the people. Faces look out at me from the past – toil-worn faces radiant with love and confidence. Nothing of what men foolishly call success is worth comparison with the experiences which those faces recall. This exceeding great reward of ministry is within your reach, and it is the best thing you can have – far better than prominence, and great office, and the applause of crowds and senates. I suppose that, after all these years, I may speak to you, not only with the authority of my Apostolic office, but also with the added authority

[1] This charge was delivered in 1936.

of long and varied experience. I say to you then — love God and love your people. Count nothing excessive which you can do for them. Serve them in your office for the love of Christ, and they will surely give you back more than you can give them. "Give, and it shall be given unto you: good measure, pressed down, shaken together, running over, shall they give into your bosom. For with what measure ye mete, it shall be measured to you again."

I think now, looking back over the years, that, though all the conditions of religious ministry have become more difficult and perplexing, and though the clergyman's office no more commands the kind of deference from society which it did when first I became a clergyman, yet a sincere man, loving Christ and his brethren, can do more good as a clergyman than in any other position. But all depends on the spirit with which that office is regarded, and the ends to which it is made serviceable. Go forward then on this great venture in the name of the Lord: go forward with humble minds, yet with a glad heart. Though the forces against you are powerful and threatening, yet it is still with you, as it was with the Hebrew prophet, that the forces of heaven gather to your prayer. "Elisha prayed, and said, Lord, I pray Thee, open his eyes that he may see. And the Lord opened the eyes of the young man; and he saw: and, behold, the mountain was full of horses and chariots of fire round about Elisha."

XII

On the eve of your ordination, I must, as is my custom, address to you some words of counsel, which may, perhaps, stay in your minds, and be of service to you in years to come, when your ordination lies behind you in the past. I propose to speak to you shortly about the Christian ministry, which you are to receive as the duty and trust of your lives. And I take, as the best description of that ministry which I can find, that which S. Peter gave in his exhortation to the presbyters of Asia. Let me read his words to you, and then add a few comments. You will find the passage in the fifth chapter of the First General Epistle, and it runs thus:

"The elders therefore among you I exhort, who am a fellow-elder, and a witness of the sufferings of Christ, who am also a partaker of the glory that shall be revealed: Tend the flock of God which is among you, exercising the oversight, not of constraint, but willingly, according unto God; nor yet for filthy lucre, but of a ready mind; neither as lording it over the charge allotted to you, but making yourselves ensamples to the flock. And when the Chief Shepherd shall be manifested, ye shall receive the crown of glory that fadeth not away. Likewise, ye younger, be subject unto the elder. Yea, all of you gird yourselves with humility, to serve one another: for God resisteth the proud, but giveth grace to the humble. Humble yourselves therefore under the mighty hand of God, that He may exalt you in due time; casting all your anxiety upon Him, because He careth for you. Be sober, be watchful: your adversary the devil, as a roaring lion, walketh about, seeking whom he may devour: whom withstand stedfast in your faith, knowing that the same sufferings are accomplished in your brethren who are in the world. And the God of all grace who called you unto His eternal glory in Christ, after that ye have suffered a little while, shall Himself perfect, stablish, strengthen you. To Him be the dominion for ever and ever. Amen."

In this passage we have two titles of the Christian minister. He is described as an elder or presbyter. Probably at that early time the notion of seniority generally held. Those were ordained to be the ministers of the Christian body who had won the confidence of their brethren, and taken the lead among them. These would most often be the older members of the Church. But even then the notion of seniority was yielding to that of official authority, as we may see in the instance of S. Timothy, who while clearly exercising an authority which might fairly be called episcopal, is bidden to let none "despise his youth." The minister is also described as a pastor or shepherd, whose primary duty is to "tend" and "feed" the flock of Christ. You will know that the word "priest" is never applied to the

Christian minister in the New Testament, or, we may add, in the earliest Christian writers. "The only priests," observes Bishop Lightfoot, "designated as such in the New Testament, are the saints, the members of the Christian brotherhood." If, indeed, the word priest were used in its proper etymological meaning, as an abbreviated form of "presbyter," much confusion of thought would have been avoided. When the Puritans objected to the use of the word in the Prayer Book, Archbishop Whitgift swept aside their objection as frivolous, because, he said, every educated man knew that priest was the same word, and carried the same sense as presbyter. You may read in Bishop Lightfoot's famous "Dissertation on the Christian Ministry" – which, though written more than sixty years ago, still is, in my judgment, the most adequate and satisfying treatment of the subject – how, by degrees, the conception of the presbyter was sacerdotalised, so that the term "priest" came to mean what the Greeks meant by *hiereus*, and you will learn also with what reservations that term may rightly be used of the Christian minister. To-night, I do not desire to embark on a discussion which is connected with such acute controversy, but I will make this single observation, that, as a safe principle for the clergyman's guidance, he may accept that which makes the New Testament the norm of his teaching. We cannot go far wrong if we are careful to maintain in our work and thought the proportion of the Apostolic Witness; and, with respect to this matter of the Christian ministry, we shall not be mistaken if, with the Apostles, we think of ourselves mainly as pastors, preachers, stewards, the servants of the people for Christ's sake. To-night I desire to fasten your attention to the thought of ourselves as ordained and commissioned to be pastors of the flock of Christ.

This word "pastor" or "shepherd" was used by the Greeks of their secular rulers, and the Jews applied it in their Scriptures to the Almighty. Jehovah was the Shepherd of Israel. "The Lord is my shepherd; I shall not want," sings the psalmist in the most familiar and most loved of the Psalms. The Lord Jesus adopted it as His own description, and illustrated it by the most tender and beautiful of all His parables, the Parable of the Lost Sheep. It is surely, of all the names by which the Christian minister has been known among men, that which is most authoritative, most befitting, and richest in spiritual suggestion. It evidently commended itself as such to the thought of the Primitive Church. "The earliest and most important of all Christian symbols" is the Good Shepherd, generally pictured with the recovered sheep on His shoulders. It is surely not without a melancholy significance that when, in the IVth century, theological controversy prevailed, this symbol was given up in the Eastern

Church. A harsher conception of the Redeemer filled the minds of His followers, and to this day the stern portrait of the Judge in the Byzantine Churches banishes the more tender and more representative view of the Lord. In the Western Church the idea of Sacrifice was supreme, and, in the gathering gloom of the Dark Ages, the tortured Figure on the Cross filled the vision of believers. Not the Good Shepherd, but the gaunt and terrible Crucifix, was the chosen symbol of the Son of Man. At the close of the Middle Ages, the pastoral character of the Christian minister had been completely submerged in the sacerdotal. It was as a "sacrificing priest" that men thought of the clergyman. This view was paramount in the medieval ordinals, and was expressed in the official vestments. At the Reformation the Church of England recovered the half-forgotten conception of the minister of Christ as the pastor of the flock. I need not remind you that this aspect is everywhere expressed in the English ordinal. The priestly character is not indeed absent and, in the actual formula of the priest's ordination, is even emphasised, but the general effect of the changes made in the service was to subordinate the sacerdotal, and to exalt the pastoral character of ministry. We cannot doubt that in all this the Church of England was divinely guided, and we shall do well if we loyally follow its guidance. Like the Primitive Church we shall accept as our favourite symbol of the Redeemer that gracious and tender figure of the Good Shepherd, bearing on His shoulders the sheep which had been lost, and which He, at so great pains and labour, had found. This pastoral character was given to the clergy by the Master Himself. He is the "Chief Shepherd" and He fulfils His pastorate on earth in and through His ordained representatives. The words which, after the Resurrection, He addressed to S. Peter, are in S. Peter's person addressed to the Christian ministry of which the Apostle was the embodiment – "Feed my lambs: Tend my sheep: Feed my sheep." Thus the Apostolic commission, which S. Peter might seem to have forfeited by his threefold apostasy, was at once restored and interpreted by a thrice-repeated pastoral charge. Most fitly are these words inscribed on the beautiful pastoral staff which was presented to Bishop Lightfoot for the use of the bishops of Durham. Jesus described Himself as "The Good Shepherd," and, in Him, we must perceive and know what spiritual pastorate really means. The passage from S. Peter's Epistle, which I read as a text, does but draw out the contents of the pastoral conception of ministry. You will note particularly three points which are emphasised.

I. *The Pastor's service must be willing* – "Not of constraint but willingly." The clergyman, in the common phrase, "must have his heart in his work." If it shall so happen that his heart goes elsewhere, then his work ceases to have reality. For the law holds that "where thy treasure is there will thy heart be also," and, when once the clergyman begins to absorb himself in other concerns, his true work to which he pledged himself at his ordination, is banished from the sanctuary of his heart. Experience attests clearly enough, on every plane of human activity, that the primary condition of efficiency is, that a man should put his heart into his work. But this is most fully the case when the work in question is the highest kind of work – spiritual ministry, the cure of souls. Slave labour failed mainly because of its proved inefficiency. And there is no slave labour so utterly worthless as that which is rendered by the slave of mammon in the character and with the profession, of the servant of Christ. "Ye cannot serve God and mammon," said Christ.

II. *The Pastor's service must be disinterested* – "Nor yet for filthy lucre, but of a ready mind." Here we touch on a very difficult but most important matter. The dualism of human nature is in the Christian ministry sharply, aggressively, presented. The clergyman has all the normal human needs. He too must earn his living. He too may have family responsibilities. He also must consent to have his work measured and remunerated on currently accepted assumptions of value and efficiency. Yet he is committed to a supernatural task. He is pledged to preach and to practise an other-worldly life. His family life has somehow to be made congruous with his ministry. His work is quite remote from the common measures, and cannot possibly be weighed in the scales of the market. You cannot really put a money value on spiritual service. Maintenance at his work is the clergyman's obvious right, maintenance of such a kind as shall secure, so far as security is possible, his efficient performance of duty. Payment for his work in terms of income no clergyman can claim, for the simple reason that no equitable determination of rates or scales of payment is possible. The popular fashion of comparing clergymen's incomes with the incomes of other descriptions of workers is really futile, and it lends itself to perilous misconceptions. We have heard far too much within recent years about the poverty of the clergy. It has encouraged a mendicant and discontented temper among the clergy, and tends to puzzle and alienate the laity. I was struck by some observations in a recent issue of the *Church Assembly News*, which strike a note of not superfluous warning; the writer is Canon J. W. Brady Moore, Rural Dean of Andover, and this is what he says:

"During my own experience (mostly in country places, I admit) since ordination forty years ago, I have found no case of what could be called real poverty amongst my brother clergy with anything approaching exactitude. I would say on the other hand that the average clergyman with his life tenure of a freehold house, £6 or £7 a week, and time which is largely at his own disposal as regards work, is relatively and proportionally in a very much better position than most other salaried professions – and he is a rich man compared to the majority of the working classes whom he is professedly supposed to serve."

Broadly I think this is true; and I am sure that the credit of the clergy, which must needs reflect itself in their spiritual influence, has been grievously injured during recent years by the unwise and exaggerated emphasis on the alleged poverty of the clergy.

III. *The Pastor's service must be humble* – "Neither as lording it over the charge allotted to you, but making yourselves ensamples to the flock." "Humility" might almost be called the Christian virtue *par excellence*, and therefore its presence in the Christian minister is indispensable. The ancient world did not include this virtue in its hierarchy of moral excellences. "Magnanimity" the ancients honoured. That was the essential quality of the hero, the "great-souled" man. But "humility" seemed in their eyes despicable. Even now the enemies of Christ's religion speak scornfully of its "slave morality." The popular conception of the clergyman does not emphasise robustness as his outstanding characteristic, and, indeed, S. Peter insists on "humility" very earnestly: "gird yourselves with humility to serve one another: for God resisteth the proud, but giveth grace to the humble." Humility has nothing to do with timidity, time-serving, and cowardice, though all these contemptible caricatures often pass for it in society. But it is the very opposite of pride, arrogance, and self-assertion. The humble Christian rarely talks about his "rights," but is very unyielding about his "duties." He is ever very ready to surrender his "interests," but he will be firm as adamant in the matter of his "religion." He knows himself to belong to the Church of the Martyrs, and to serve a Master who will tolerate no rival. "Humility" is always connected with a just knowledge of self, and with a readiness to serve others. It disallows the censorious habit, which is relentlessly severe on a brother's fault, while serenely unconscious of one's own. It has ever the warning words of Christ in mind: "Why beholdest thou the mote that is in thy brother's eye, but considerest not the beam that is in thine own eye? Thou hypocrite, cast out first the beam out of thine own eye, and then shalt thou see clearly to cast out the mote out of thy brother's eye." The ground tones of the humble Christian's character are audible in the lowly prayer of the publican, who yet was justified rather than the Pharisee, "God, be merciful to me a sinner."

"Humility" is inseparable from the spirit of service. There was a memorable occasion in the Saviour's life when He found Himself confronted by a sudden explosion of jealous ambition among His disciples, and rebuked it by a significant reference to Himself: "Jesus called them to Him, and saith unto them, Ye know that they which are accounted to rule over the Gentiles lord it over them; and their great ones exercise authority over them. But it is not so among you: but whosoever would become great among you, shall be your minister: and whosoever would be first among you, shall be servant of all. For verily the Son of Man came not to be ministered unto, but to minister, and to give His life a ransom for many." The temptation of all who are entrusted with office is to treat the respect due to their position as if it were a homage due to themselves. This temptation is, perhaps, more formidable in the early days of inexperience and obscurity than in later life, when the years have taught much which the days never knew, and there is comparatively small risk of being misled into over-estimating the significance of place and power. The best and only adequate cure for clerical vanity is a deep devotion to the Divine Master. "We preach not ourselves, but Christ Jesus as Lord," said that prince of pastors, S. Paul, and he was able to add "and ourselves as your servants for Jesus' sake."

It is difficult to overstate the injury to religion which has flowed from the spring of clerical pride. So frequent has the combination of public office and personal arrogance been in the experience of Christendom, that the extremer forms of human pride are habitually associated with priests, prelates, and pontiffs. What has been a conspicuous scandal on the great scenes of history has been but too common in the petty annals of the parishes. Be on your guard against this fault. It was the salutary custom of the ancient Romans to check the exultation of the victorious general, to whom they allotted the honour of a triumph, by placing in his chariot a slave charged to whisper in his ear at intervals, as his procession passed in its pride and pomp through the streets of the capital, the chastening reminder, *Memento et tu es homo*. Well for us if our own conscience can be trusted to do the humbling work of the Roman slave, when we are puffed up by some little prominence or popularity which may come to us. Even if, which may not be the case, we have gifts which are exceptional, and achieve a larger measure of success than falls to most men, why should we be vain? "For who maketh thee to differ? And what hast thou that thou didst not receive? But if thou didst receive it, why dost thou glory, as if thou hadst not received it?"

The reward, of which S. Peter speaks, has little to do with the kind of professional success which men covet on earth – office, popular applause, social influence. Even in those early days of danger and conflict, the lure of these things was beginning to bear badly on Christian ministers. The Apostle's warnings against "filthy lucre" and pride of office show that the door was already opening for the great scandals of ecclesiastical history. The reward of the faithful minister is quite other than the world values, or worldly minded men imagine. It is the recognition and acceptance of the servant by the Lord, whose commission he had received, and whose cause he had maintained. "When the Chief Shepherd shall be manifested, ye shall receive the crown of glory that fadeth not away." That is the loyal clergyman's reward in the great day of final reckoning, to hear the Master's word: "Well done, good and faithful servant, thou hast been faithful. Enter thou into the joy of thy Lord."